Recreations and Studies of A Country clergyman of the Eighteenth Century

Thomas Twining

BIBLIOLIFE

RECREATIONS AND STUDIES

OF

A COUNTRY CLERGYMAN

OF THE

EIGHTEENTH CENTURY

BEING SELECTIONS FROM THE CORRESPONDENCE

OF THE

REV. THOMAS TWINING, M.A.

TRANSLATOR OF 'ARISTOTLE ON POETRY'

SOMETIME RECTOR OF ST MARY'S, COLCHESTER) AND FORMERLY FELLOW OF
SIDNEY SUSSEX COLLEGE, CAMBRIDGE

LONDON

JOHN MURRAY, ALBEMARLE STREET

1882

PREFACE.

In placing before the public the present records of the life and correspondence of my great-uncle, the Rev. Thomas Twining, sometime Rector of St Mary's, Colchester, of whom the memory—dear on all accounts to his family—still lives among scholars by his work on 'Aristotle on Poetry,' I am prepared for the question, what can have moved me to publish that which has been reserved for nearly a century for the private use of the family.

The best answer to that enquiry will, I hope, be found in the work itself, believing, as I do, that notwithstanding the lapse of time and the passing away of the entire generation of those who rejoiced in personal intercourse with and devoted attachment to the subject of this memoir, it will still be a satisfaction to a new generation of the family to have a more accessible record of an ancestor whom they have so much reason to revere ; while to the

public at large—notably to men of letters, lovers of
art and music, and to all who can appreciate a vast
fund of playful humour—a perusal of the following
pages can hardly fail to be attractive.   The sketches
of home scenery, and the contrasts afforded between
the leisurely journeying of those times, along the old
coach-roads of the country, and the ' express ' movements of the present day, may also not be without
interest.

    Some explanation, however, may still be required
of the circumstances which have led to the publication
having been so long deferred.   They are these.   My
grandfather, the half-brother of the Rev. Thomas
Twining, his constant correspondent and frequent
companion, and so the best qualified in all respects
to have done justice to the undertaking, was prevented
by severe and long-protracted illness from completing
the work of preparation, in which he had made considerable progress.   In that labour of love he had
had the advantage of the willing and able assistance
of many surviving and attached friends, whose names
have been gratefully recorded by him in the following
memoir—Dr. Parr, Dr. Burney, Dr. Charles Burney,
Dr. John Hey (sometime Norrisian Professor at Cambridge), and Dr. and Mrs. Hughes ; the latter devoting
herself with loving assiduity to the transcription of
the original documents for the press.   In the next

succeeding generation the work was carried forward by the Rev. Daniel Twining, the nephew and literary executor of the Rev. Thomas Twining In the latter capacity he had taken an active interest in the undertaking from the first, and had brought his ripe scholarship and critical taste to bear upon it with constant zeal. Much was accomplished in the arrangement of the materials, but he could never sufficiently satisfy himself to go to press ; and in 1853, shortly before his decease, he made over the charge of all the letters and papers to myself. Thus it has fallen to my lot, in such intervals of leisure as a busy life has afforded, to complete a work for which others had made so much thoughtful preparation.

The responsibility for the act of publication rests entirely on myself : whatever credit may attach to the work is wholly due to those who preceded me in the task. It only remains for me to add the expression of my earnest hope that, in bringing before the public the following records of a blameless, simple, and learned life, I may be doing no wrong either to the memory of the ancestor whom I desire to honour, or to the wishes of those members of his family and friends who survived him in his generation.

RICHARD TWINING

215 STRAND .
March, 1882

CONTENTS.

MEMOIR

SELECTIONS FROM THE LETTERS AND NOTE-BOOKS OF THE REV. T. TWINING.

CONTENTS.

MISCELLANIES.

MEMOIR

BY RICHARD TWINING, THE BROTHER AND CON-
TEMPORARY OF THE REV. THOMAS TWINING

Written in 1817.

———•◦•———

A LIFE spent chiefly in studious retirement is not
likely to afford many anecdotes which would either
interest or amuse the public, and in this way was by
far the greater part of my brother's life spent. But
when distinguished literary attainments are the result
of such retirement, and when the most amiable conduct in private life can also be adduced, even a few
anecdotes, a short history, of such a person, may be
thought not wholly unworthy of attention from the
public.

Thomas Twining, born January 8, 1735, was the
eldest son of Mr. Daniel Twining, tea dealer, of
London. He was intended by his father for his own
business, and was placed at a small school at Twickenham, where his father resided. At this school he
learnt but little, as I have often heard him declare.
He was afterwards actually placed in his father's
business. Here he was very unhappy. His aversion
to such a situation, his unfitness for it, soon became

B

evident ; his passion for books, provided they were not books of business, was equally manifest. His father therefore determined to indulge his taste for literary pursuits by sending him to the University. To prepare him for going thither, he was placed under the private care and in the family of the Rev. Palmer Smythies, of Colchester. From this place, in 1755, he was removed to Sidney Sussex College, Cambridge, where he was elected a foundation scholar in 1756. He took the degrees of B.A. in 1760, and M.A. in 1763. He was a candidate for the clas-sical medals ; and, though not a successful candidate, he acquired upon his examination a high degree of credit, and was always placed by those who best knew him in the foremost rank of classical scholars. He applied himself, indeed, with great diligence to his studies ; to them he devoted not only a large portion of the day, but also a considerable part of the night. In December 1760 he was elected a Fellow of his college, and during his residence was appointed to several distinguished offices.

My brother's musical talent discovered itself at a very early age, and it met with encouragement from his father, who was himself a performer, though by no means a distinguished performer, on the violoncello and the organ ; and also from Mr. Stanley, with whom his father was intimate. My brother performed ex-tremely well upon the violin before he went to Cambridge, and during his residence there bore a conspicuous part in the oratorios, and at other musical meetings.

His residence at the University was shortened in consequence of an attachment which he formed before he went to it. Whilst he was at Colchester, under the care of Mr. Smythies, Miss Smythies, his daughter, was my brother's fellow-pupil ; they learnt Latin and Greek at the same time, and, being nearly of an age, it is not surprising that an attachment took place between the young students. They were married in January 1764, and they settled at Fordham, near Colchester, where my brother had the ' sole charge.' The parsonage house, in which he resided nearly thirty years (as he himself says in one of his letters, ' the happiest years of his life '), was old and irregular, but sufficiently convenient. And his study—the room in which he spent the most part of his time—was extremely cheerful and pleasant, looking into a garden of sweets. During his long residence in this place his favourite pursuits were rarely interrupted. Few men, I believe, possessed or enjoyed complete tranquillity more than he did. Nor was it broken in upon by domestic concerns. How much he wished to leave them to the entire management of his wife will appear by the following passage from Tibullus, which he wrote in the first leaf of her account book—

Elizabeth Twining,
Jan. 21, 1764.
. . . ' illi sint omnia curæ,
Et juvet in tota me nihil esse domo.

Her good sense and cheerfulness rendered her a most excellent companion for my brother, and though her long and severe illness prepared him in a considerable degree for the loss of her, he felt that loss most acutely. She died in 1796.

His talents and acquirements certainly enabled him to bear a conspicuous part in the society of literary men , yet in large companies (in mixed society) he was generally silent. He had some intimate friends to whom his powers of conversation were well known ; and his learning, his taste, his playful humour, the total absence of everything like pretension or affectation, and, above all, his great tenderness and simplicity of heart, rendered him no less delightful as their companion than amiable as their friend.

In the constant habits of his life, and in the performance of all the duties of a clergyman, particularly of the most important duties of the minister of a parish, he was exemplary. He never lost sight of that behaviour which became his position. His unaffected piety, the regularity of all the habits of his life, the suavity of his manners, and the serious and excellent manner in which he performed the service of his church—all these circumstances obtained for him the love and confidence of his parishioners both at Fordham, where he passed so many years, and at St. Mary's at Colchester, during that shorter residence which was terminated by his death. He had two small livings, viz. the Vicarage of White Notley, in

Essex, which was given to him by Bishop Terrick in the year 1772, and the Rectory of St. Mary's in Colchester, for which he was indebted to another Bishop of London (Porteus), whom he remembered at Cambridge.

It will not, I trust, be deemed improper if, in this brief account of my brother's peaceable and adventureless life, I should just notice those friendships which contributed most materially to the comfort of it. His intimacy with the late Rev. Dr. Hey, who was Norrisian Professor at Cambridge, and the Rev. Mr. Elmsall, commenced at the University, and was uninterrupted during their lives. Of the accurate, the amiable, the candid Dr. Hey it is unnecessary for me to say anything. He is, and will be, known by his works, and at present he is remembered with esteem and affection by many persons living. He and my brother met frequently. Mr. Elmsall,[1] their common friend, resided after the year 1772 at a greater distance, at Emley, near Wakefield. Their meetings were of necessity less frequent. To mitigate the evil of separation as well as they could, they agreed to correspond with each other at stated periods—I believe alternate months. It may seem strange to any one who considers this circumstance, that none of my brother's letters to Mr. Elmsall appear in this collection. I lament that they do not, for such was

[1] The Rev. Henry Elmsall, Rector of Emley, near Wakefield, died December 6, 1797.

the similarity of taste between these friends, and such
the perfect freedom of their intercourse, that my
brother's epistolary talent would have appeared to
great advantage from this correspondence But I
have reason to think that his letters were destroyed
immediately after Mr. Elmsall's death. I cannot refrain from adducing in this place a few words from
a letter which my brother wrote to me in 1797, on
the death of Mr Elmsall :—' Hey and I must feel
this loss as long as we live. But I am thankful that
I have enjoyed for so many years the acquaintance
and friendship of such a man. The recollection of it
will be dear to me as long as I live. In strong un-
prejudiced sense of judgment I think he was superior
to any man I have ever known ; in humour beyond
any , and a more virtuous man, I verily believe, never
lived—a man more *perfectly* free from his youth from
every shade of vice.'

Amongst my brother's Colchester friends, the Rev.
Dr. Nathaniel Forster held undoubtedly the first
place. He was a man of a vigorous and comprehen-
sive, and, if I may be allowed the expression, *prac-
tical* understanding. He was upon almost all occasions, either of a private or public nature, both able
and willing to give valuable counsel to those who
applied to him for it. My brother's literary communications with him were of the most unreserved
and satisfactory kind possible. These two friends
enjoyed, though for too short a time, a most valuable

addition to their society in Dr. Parr. *Then* could
Colchester boast of the ' noctes cœnæque Deûm.'
But Dr. Parr quitted the Free School of Colchester
for that of Norwich ; from which place he removed
into Warwickshire, to a still greater distance ; so that
from the time of Dr Parr's leaving Colchester, he and
my brother met but seldom, I may venture to say to
their mutual mortification. The friendly intercourse
between the late Dr. Burney and my brother formed
an important feature in his life. Their love of music
rendered them most apt companions for each other.
Nothing was wanting but an opportunity of bringing
them together. Fortune, who is not always so well
employed, performed this kind office. They were far
from young when they met, and they could ill afford
to lose time They soon became intimate, they soon
became friends. Much is often, and justly, said
against sudden intimacies and hastily formed friendships ; but in the present instance the intimacy had a
solid foundation, the friendship was pure, and lasted
as long as their lives. At the precise time of their
first meeting, Dr. Burney was engaged in his valuable
and laborious work, ' The History of Music,' and he
was in the most difficult part of it, the history of
ancient music I should not, perhaps, go too far if
I were to say that he could not have found any person
who was better qualified to afford him substantial
and pleasant service than my brother. Both in theory
and practice he was a good musician. It happened

also, that he was well prepared to give immediate help, for he had actually had in contemplation a work of a similar nature. He had read, with his usual perseverance and accuracy, much upon the subject, and his commonplace book was well stored with materials. As soon, however, as he became acquainted with Dr. Burney and his plan, he cheerfully offered all the aid in his power. 'I like the man, and I like the subject upon which he is engaged,' was a remark which my brother made to me; and I am sure that he had as much pleasure in giving, as Dr. Burney could possibly have in receiving, assistance. They corresponded frequently, and met occasionally. My brother often spoke with delight of the visit which Dr. Burney paid him at his quiet residence at Fordham. At the time to which I am alluding, Dr. Burney was much occupied by professional engagements. My brother was rich in leisure. The pleasant manner in which each contributed information, and each where they happened to differ maintained his own opinion, might almost be considered as a model for the literary correspondence of friends. I am much indebted to Dr. Burney's son, the Rev. Charles Burney, for the very kind and liberal manner in which he put into my hands a large collection of my brother's letters to his father.

If the principle of noticing in this slight sketch of my brother's life those circumstances which materially affected the happiness of it be admitted, it will cer-

tainly be right to mention his intimacy with my most
valued friends, the Rev. Dr. Hughes (Canon Resi-
dentiary of St. Paul's) and Mrs. Hughes. It was
owing to their hospitable and tempting invitations
that he visited North Wales, and they accompanied
him upon a tour through some of the finest parts
of that romantic country. He was a great admirer
of rural scenery. Upon his visits to his friend Mr.
Elmsall, in the West Riding of Yorkshire, he had
been much struck by the rich and beautiful views
with which that neighbourhood abounds. In some
of his letters he describes them. He had also been
at Matlock, with which he was delighted. The
scenery was more romantic than any that he had
then beheld. But North Wales at once astonished
and delighted him with its more wild and more sublime pictures. I was of the party on this tour, and I
had the pleasure of witnessing the impressions—they
might be called *first* impressions—which such scenery
made upon him. The recollection of them continued
to give him pleasure to the end of life.

My brother's translation of Aristotle on 'Poetry,'
with copious notes and two original dissertations, is
well known to scholars ; and, I may safely add, has
been generally approved by them. From such I could
adduce testimonies in its favour, but it is not necessary
for me to do so. He published also three sermons.
One of them was a visitation sermon which he preached
before the Bishop of London in the year 1790, 'On

the Abuse of Reason, as Applied to the Mysterious
Doctrines of Revelation.' This sermon is out of print,
and I shall probably comply with a request which
has been made to me to reprint it. The subject of
another sermon was 'The Duty of Allegiance.' This
sermon was preached before the Corporation of Colchester in September 1794, and was printed at their
request. The remaining sermon was preached and
published, for the benefit of the Sunday schools in
Colchester, in June 1787. His health evidently de-
clined during the last year or two of his life, but he
did not suffer under any acute disorder. He died in
his parsonage house at Colchester on August 6, 1804,
and was buried at Mile End, near Colchester, where
his wife and many of her family had been interred.
Dr. Parr, in testimony of his friendship for my
brother, and of the high opinion which he entertained
of him as a scholar, most kindly offered to write his
epitaph.[1] It is placed in his church at Colchester. I
shall subjoin the epitaph. It would not become me
to praise it ; suitable and acceptable praise must
come from the 'laudato viro.' I must, however, express my sense of the obligation which I am under to
Dr. Parr ; and at the same time my regret that the
inscription is not placed where it would be more fre-

---

[1] Dr. Parr's opinion of his friend may be also gathered from
the words which he wrote in his 'presentation' copy of Twining's
Aristotle '—' The gift of the author, whom I am proud and happy to
call my friend, because he is one of the best scholars now living, and
one of the best men that ever lived —July 7, 1790.'

quently read by those who are qualified to appreciate its merit, and to learn from it, as such readers could not fail of doing, the literary attainments and the virtues which it records.

RICHARD TWINING.

February 1817.

Extracts from a Letter from Dr. Parr.

Dec. 2, 1816.

DEAR SIR,— . . . . I consider your brother as possessing a talent for epistolary writing certainly not surpassed by any of his contemporaries—wit, sagacity, learning, languages ancient and modern, the best principles of criticism, and the most exquisite feelings of taste, all united their various force and various beauty. Whether he wielded an argument, or tossed about an opinion, all was natural, original, and most delightful. In his remarks on solemn coxcombs, pert sciolists, churlish pedants, and intolerant bigots, he brought into my mind what was once said by a most competent judge, by a most eloquent writer, on these subjects · ' Me quidem hercule valde illa movent stomachosa et quasi submorosa ridicula non cum a moroso dicuntur, tunc enim non sal, sed natura ridetur' (Cic. *De Orat.* ii. 69).

Your brother was not morose; ' quia amari sales' were strangers to his mind and his pen. Mr. Twining, no critic of his day excelled your brother Thomas ;

he understood Greek and Latin, and he wrote perfect English.   I have many letters of his, and they are most precious in my sight.   But they are in vast confused masses, and I have not leisure to look them up.   No ; I mean to have them carefully preserved. But, were it otherwise, I would not communicate them for publication.   I know my own situation, and I never will do by my correspondents what I should resent their doing by me.   I could not trust my own judgment or my own humour, in separating that which ought from that which ought not to see the light.   Thomas, when he wrote to Nathaniel Forster, or Samuel Parr, never thought of the Press.   Thank you for promising to let me see the letters in which my name happens to be mentioned ; let me see them, and I will tell you my real mind.   Indeed, sir, I think it a real and a high honour to have been the friend and correspondent of Thomas Twining, and in forming my determination I will not be squeamish or vain.

Take care of your health.   Give my very best compliments to Richard and all your family, and believe me your faithful well wisher and respectful humble servant,

(Signed)   S. PARR.

Hatton, Dec. 2, 1816.

THOMÆ TWINING A.M.

Hujus Ecclesiæ Rectori

Viro in quo

Doctrina inerat multiplex et recondita

Ingenium elegans et acutum

Scribendi genus non exile spinosumque

Sed accuratum et exquisitum

In rebus quæ ad artem criticam pertinent explicandis

Sermo sine aculeo et maledictis facetus

Et sapore pæne proprio Athenarum imbutus

Mansuetudo morum et comitas suis perjucunda

Pietas erga Deum pura atque sincera

Siquidem honesta de natura ejus opinione

Stabilique in Christo fide potissimum nixa est

Et cum summa in omnes homines benevolentia

Nunquam non conjuncta

Ricardus Twining Fratri carissimo

Nato VIII Calend. Januar. anno sacro MDCCXXXV

Mortuo VIII ID. August. MDCCCIV

Condito Colcestriæ in sepulcreto templi

Ad Mileend siti

H.M.P.C.

SELECTIONS FROM THE LETTERS AND NOTE-BOOKS OF THE Rev. T. TWINING.

————◆————

GREEK MUSIC AND MUSICAL INSTRUMENTS. — BURETTE'S 'DISSERTATIONS.'—CHURCH MUSIC.

To the Rev. Mr. Mainwaring,[1] *at Warlingham, near Croydon.*

Cambridge, Jan 1761.

I should be much ashamed of having so long deferred an answer to your letter, if I had not an excuse to make which I hope will appear to you, as it does to me, a reasonable one. The truth is, I really could not find time to consider the matter about which you wrote, nor to read the dissertations you mentioned to me till I had got over the usual trouble of an examination[2] for a Fellowship, which with us is not to be had without a smattering of Hebrew.

Nothing can be more consistent with the constant course of blundering for which the critical reviewers are famous, than the use they have made of that passage in Aristotle's Book ' De Mundo.' It is no wonder that upon the first reading it should seem to

[1] Afterwards Margaret Professor of Divinity at Cambridge.
[2] Thomas Twining was elected a Fellow of Sidney Sussex College, December 22, 1760.

describe the harmony of different parts ; for it speaks
of a chorus of many voices singing together, and we
know of no such thing as a chorus of unisons or
octaves.   To be sure the words would serve very well
for a description of our modern chorus ; but the reviewers, before they so confidently inferred from them
the use of what *we* call harmony among the ancients,
should have proved that the passage could have no
other sense, and that their ἁρμονία and our harmony
meant the same thing.   I entirely agree with you
that the expressions ἁρμονίαν ἐμμέλη and κοροφαίου
καταραξάντος, or καταρξάντος,[1] prove nothing ; ἁρμονία is generally used by the Greeks in the same sense
as μελῳδία ; if it was ever used in our sense of the
word to denote the effect of different melodies carried
on at the same time, it would be very strange if this
did not somewhere appear in the eight (or nine) Greek
treatises written professedly on the subject.   As for
the Coryphæus, or Precentor—the leader and regu-
lator of the chorus—the use of his office is obvious
enough ; but I don't see how anything can be drawn
from it to serve the reviewers' purpose.   The words ἐν
διαφόροις φώναις ὀξυτέραις καὶ βαρυτέραις
seem most favourable to their hypothesis ; yet I have
no doubt of their meaning only (as you say) voices
of different tones and pitches ; and this sense seems

---

[1] So it is in the edition I have consulted, and I believe it is better
than καταραξάντος, because Aristotle elsewhere calls the Corophæus
ὁ κατάρχων.

to me to be confirmed by another passage in the
‘ Harmonical Problems’ of the same writer, in which
(if I am not mistaken) such a chorus as I understand
from the words in question is more precisely described. The passage is this : ‘ ἐκ παίδων γὰρ καὶ
νέων καὶ ἀνδρῶν γίνεται τὸ ἀντίφωνον· οἱ διε-
στᾶσι τοῖς τόνοις, ὡς νήτη πρὸς τὴν ὑπάτην.’
Aristotle asserts in the preceding sentence that the
ἀντιφωνία was the συμφωνία or harmony of the
octave ; *for,* says he, the ἀντίφωνον is the effect of a
chorus composed of boys, youths, and men, whose
voices differ an octave from each other in pitch ; or
as the string called Νήτη differs from Ὑπάτη. As
for ἀντίφωνον, it is defined by Greek musicians to be
only the concord of the octave or double octave, in
·contradistinction to the other concords ; viz. the
fifth, the fourth, the eleventh and twelfth, *octave and
fifth* single, and *octave and fourth* together ; all which
they denominated παράφωνα.

     After all, any simple passage of this kind taken
from an author not professedly writing upon the
subject, must be very strong and precise indeed to
overturn such an argument as the entire silence of
all the ancient treatises on music extant ; in not one
of which (as we are assured by those who have examined them, and written commentaries upon them)
is any rule given for composition in parts, or anything said from which it can be inferred that the
ancients had any knowledge of that kind. To say

that they knew nothing of *harmony*, nothing of the effect resulting from the mixture of sounds, would certainly be false. They speculated upon the different intervals of their scale, they compared sounds with each other, and settled the matter of concords, and discords, and concinnities, or imperfect concords; some by their ears, and some (as we are told) by their mathematics. But all this seems to have been used by them no otherwise than as the foundation and rule of their Melopœia; which matter M. Burette has explained, I think, very cleverly in the dissertation upon the Melopée.

Dr. Wallis gives the same account in the appendix to his edition of Ptolemy; and asserts that, as far as he could find, the ancients had no knowledge of the composition of different melodies. He allows that expressions do sometimes occur that *seem* to contradict this; but the most, he thinks, that can fairly be deduced from them is, that now and then they struck two or three strings together; but that they were used to carry on distinct parts, like bass and treble, &c., by no means appears. There is a curious chapter in Ptolemy setting forth the defects of an instrument called Μονόχορδος κανών, which appears to have been in some vogue at the time he wrote. His principal objection to it is, that from the very construction of it, it was impossible to produce two notes at once, or strike a chord upon it —μηδὲ δύο διαφερόντων ἅμα ἀπτέσθαι τόπων; so that upon this instrument, says

he, you lose the chief beauties of instrumental performance—ἐπιψάλειν, συγκρουσέως, ἀναπλόκης, κατα-
πλόκης, σύρματος, καὶ ὅλως τῆς δία τῶν ὑπερβάτων
φθογγῶν συμπλόκης ; it is not easy, indeed, to as-
certain the precise meaning of all these words, but
they seem plainly to indicate something more than
simple melody, especially the last expression, ' *the
complication of distant notes.*' But if the most be
made of this passage, I am afraid we shall have no
reason to allow the ancient lyrist any deeper skill in
composition than is requisite for the flinging in here
and there a common chord, or a sprinkle of arpeggio.

This seems to be all that we have any reason to
think of the instrumental music of the Greeks And
as to their choral, I imagine it was performed in
unisons or octaves, according as the voices of which
the chorus was composed were of the same or different
pitches But as for the blending together different
melodies even in plain counterpoint, I don't find that
there are any traces of such a practice to be (*met
with*) discovered.   After all this salmagondis of quotation, can you bear another slice of Aristotle ?   One
of his problems is, ' Why only the concord of the octave was used in singing ? '—Διάτι ἡ διαπάσων συμφωνία ἀδέται μόνη.   Now, without puzzling ourselves
about Aristotle's solution of this problem, would not
the question itself (and it seems pretty plainly put)
be nonsense, if we suppose the Greeks (at least at
that·time) to have ever sung in parts ? for I think

they could not have well done that without using the
other concords.

I was very well entertained with Monsieur Bu·· tte's
' Dissertations,' and thank you for putting them into
my hands. His account of the rhythm and melopée
of the Greeks is very clear and intelligible, and I am
sure I know too little of the matter to be able to say
that it is anywhere not right.

I find he is of the common opinion too that the
ancients knew nothing of composition in parts ; and
he refers me to some former work of his in which he
had endeavoured to prove that ; if I knew the title of
that book I would endeavour to get it, perhaps it may
be a dissertation in some other volume of the ' Histoire de l'Académie ' ; and I did once attempt to inform
myself about the Greek music from the authors
whom Mons. Burette quotes as his authorities ; and
I went on very well till I came to the modes—'ibi
omnis effusus labor!'—when I came to examine the
accounts of different authors, all was contradiction
and confusion ; ὀξὺ sometimes got below βαρὺ, and
the top of the system was the bottom.   I had not
industry enough to endeavour to set this matter to
rights, nor do I understand Mons. Burette's explanation of the modes ; but his account of the system,
the genera, &c., agrees exactly with what I had made
myself. As for the specimens of Greek music, they
are enough, I should think, to damp the keenest
curiosity that ever forced its way through a page of

Aristoxenus. I confess I am unable to see beauty in them of any kind or degree. What effect that mixed rhythm might have, I know not ; I can make nothing of it ; and still less of their sesquialterate rhythm, of which I wish they had left me an instance, which I think verily could not have been to their credit. The best specimen is the last, the beginning of an ode of Pindar; the melody is vastly simple, and tolerably natural, but certainly there is nothing to wonder at in it, except that it should not be better. Indeed, these instances of the coarseness and insipidity of the Greek air would almost persuade one to believe, against reason, that it was made amends for by some striking beauties of harmony.

I borrowed Antaniotti's book, and could not find the assertion you mention in it , and I have looked into some other treatises, but can find nothing like it. I am not able to judge at all the probability of it, but one thing strikes me: if our church music was derived from the Jews, how comes it that we know nothing of their system ?

A BUDGET OF ENGLISH NEWS.

To the Rev. John Hey (in Paris).

Fordham, October 6, 1771.

Mon cher Hey,—Voici de quoi régaler votre critique quelque affamée qu'elle puisse être, bévues, solécismes, phrases barbares, etc., mais qu'importe, enfin ?

Votre lettre m'a fait d'autant plus de plaisir qu'à la
vérité je ne m'y étois guère attendu, un certain
principe d'équité dont je ne suis pas dépourvu, et
qui fait que je me mette par fois à la place des gens,
ne m'avoit point permis d'espérer une seconde lettre,
je sentois bien à quel point le tems vous devoit être
précieux ; mais vous êtes meilleur que bon, puissiez-
vous en être récompensé en ce moment pour le
spectacle de tout ce que Paris a de plus brillant et
de plus magnifique ! Mais à propos de Paris, par
une étourderie dont assurément vous vous seriez bien
gardé dans ce climat sage et grossier, vous ne me
marquez pas le tems de votre séjour à Paris : que
deviendra ma lettre au Café de Conti si par malheur
vous n'y seriez plus ? l'idée de mon pauvre barbouillage abandonné au milieu d'un pays étranger me
fait frémir. Mais il faut bien que je vous écrive à
tout hasard, et j'écris le plutôt qu'il m'est possible
Oui, vraiment, votre délicatesse au sujet de cette
correction-là, m'a paru extraordinaire. Apparemment que si quelqu'un vous faisoit voir un trou dans
votre bas, puisque vous ne l'aviez pas reconnu vous-
même, vous n'auriez garde d'y toucher : ce seroit une
espèce de mensonge. Ah ! ce maudit *de*, vous avez
raison. Voilà encore de vos scrupules ; mais pour
ceci, passe, c'est une règle bien fondée comme règle
générale, mais dont vous fîtes bien de vous affranchir
à mon égard. Soyez désormais françois, l'affaire est
faite, loin que j'y trouve à redire, au contraire je vous

en félicite, vous n'en serez que plus à mon gré. Il y
a trop du '*bull-dog*' dans le véritable caractère
anglois, pour que je puisse me piquer trop de ma
patrie. Quant à notre constitution politique, c'est
sans doute le chef-d'œuvre de la sagesse humaine ;
peu s'en fallut qu'on ne fît main basse sur le pauvre
Alderman Nash l'autre jour ; on le fit descendre du
hustings, et sans la protection du Sheriff Wilkes, je
ne sçais ce qu'en seroit devenu. Mais quoi ! il avait
osé vouloir bien être élu Lord Mayor, s'il plaisoit
aux citoyens de l'élire. Je viens de lire une nouvelle
lettre de Junius, où en s'adressant au D. de G. il lui
demande, ' Is the union of Blifil [1] and Black George
no longer a romance ? ' Voici encore des nouvelles :
un nombre à ce qu'on me dit considérable du clergé
(mêlé de quelques médecins, etc.) ont dressé et signé
une requête, qui doit être présentée au plutôt à la
chambre des communes, et dont l'objet est de
s'affranchir du joug de la souscription aux articles et
à la liturgie. Voilà ce qu'ils ne veulent pas, et en
quoi ils sont d'accord ; on n'a qu'à les demander pré-
cisément ce qu'ils veulent, pour en faire d'abord une
confédération de sable, et ce sera sans doute le moyen
dont on se servira pour les éconduire tout doucement.
Mon Rector a signé. Voilà, n'y-a-t'il pas là un joli
petit réformateur ? Il m'a dit que l'évecque de ——
s'est déclaré chef du parti hétérodoxe, l'évecque de
—— du parti orthodoxe. Εὖ μὲν τίς δόρυ θηξάσθω, εὖ

---

[1] Vide *Tom Jones, passim.*

δ' ἄσπιδα θέσθω, etc. Après tout je doute que tout cela aille assez loin pour fournir seulement un peu d'amusement à nous autres philosophes qui savons imiter la sagesse de Gallio.

Mais cette charmante Madame Renaud : ah ! je conçois jusqu'où doit aller votre *aupisme*,[1] peu s'en fallut que je ne le partage avec vous. Mais ce qui m'a un peu surpris, c'est que vous parlez avec tant de complaisance du *chant* françois, trois chanteurs françois qui vous font plaisir dans une seule troupe, et pour comble Madame Renaud ! Il faut que Rousseau, Burney, etc. exagéroient un peu le mauvais goût de l'exécution françoise. On croiroit à les entendre qu'elle fut un supplice pour tout autre qu'un françois. Quant au genre actuel de leur musique théatrale, ou plutôt de leur drame lyrique, je ne sçais si je me trompe, mais il me paroît d'un style très supérieur à celui de nos opéras anglois. Je devinai donc juste et c'étoit le *Confitebor* que vous me faites plaisir en me la procurant ; un certain verset m'en a paru charmant, j'en ai perdu toute idée, mais j'aurai grand plaisir à le retrouver. Il faut avouer pourtant qu'il ne se trouve pas . . . . . de plus mal entendu que le choix des paroles, qui (*words torn out of the original*) ne méritoient guère une meilleure (*a word torn out*) apparemment que celle de leur auteur. Ne manquez pas, je vous supplie, de me l'ap-

[1] *Dupisme* used to mean being enamoured : perhaps it got that sense from some particular innamorato being a *Dupe.*—J. H.

porter ; c'est *in quarto* de Diderot, que vous m'indiquez.
Je le dévorerai avidement ; il y a longtems que je
suis fou de ces livres-là.   La comédie de Jenner
s'appelle ' The Man of Family,' elle ne me plaît
point ; voilà une dédicace beaucoup trop dédicace à
Garrick, et puis une préface où le *focus irati* est
exposé tout nud aux yeux de tout le monde de la
façon la plus impudique.   C'est un homme qui se
promène en public la culotte ouverte sans qu'il s'en
doute.   Je lis à présent ' Recherches sur les Améri-
càins,' par M. de P., c'est un livre intéressant par son
objet, plein de faits très curieux et de réflexions
philosophiques et sensées.   Trouvez, si vous le pouvez,
qui est ce M. de P.   Je voudrai aussi savoir ce que
l'on pense en France du ' Système de la Nature,'
qu'on dit être l'ouvrage de plusieurs des meilleurs
écrivains françois, Diderot entr'autres.   C'est une
défense ouverte de l'Athéisme, je n'ai pu ni le voir
ni l'acheter.   Jenny S. se porte bien.   Madame T.
se pique d'embonpoint françois.   Elle vous fait ses
complimens.   Les femmes ne se mêlent que peu de
géographie.   C'est assez que vous ayez séjourné
quelques mois hors d'Angleterre, pour qu'elle s'attend,
dit-elle, à vous revoir le visage basané et ridé, etc.
Pour moi, je serois contraint malgré moi de me
rendre à Cambridge pour vous excéder de questions,
boire à la santé de Madame Renaud, vous voir enfin
danser, tirer des armes, et *avoir l'air raisonnable.*   Je
suis toujours votre ami

                                        T. T.

THE HARPSICHORD AND THE PIANOFORTE.

To Dr. Burney.

Colchester, April 4, 1774.

I find there is no end of waiting here in town for the great and long uninterrupted mornings of the country. I therefore snatch my pen in a passion, and resolve to keep scrawling something to you, with or without thought, sense, or nonsense, as it happens. It requires no thought to thank you heartily, in the first place, for all the trouble you have so kindly taken about my pianoforte.[1] It arrived safe at the proper time, without being even much put out of tune by the jumble. I am much pleased with the tone of it, which is sweet and even; in the pianissimo it is charming. Altogether the instrument is delightful, and I play upon it *con amore*, and with the pleasure I expected. If it has defects which a good harpsichord has not, it has beauties and delicacies which amply compensate, and which make the harpsichord wonderfully flashy and insipid when played after it; though for some purposes, and in some of my musical moods, though not the best I confess, I might turn to the harpsichord in preference. There are times when one's ear calls only for harmony, and a pleasant jingle; when one is disposed to merely sensual music, that tickles the auditory nerves, and does not disturb the indolence of our feelings or imagination. But as soon

[1] The first piano used in England was in a performance of the 'Beggar's Opera,' at Covent Garden, 1767.

as ever my spirit wakes, as soon as my heart-strings
catch the gentlest vibration, I swivel me round incon-
tinently to the pianoforte.

ANCIENT MUSIC AND DRAMATIC ART.—RECITATIVE
AND ELOCUTION.—LAWES AND PURCELL —COUN-
TRY LIFE.

To Dr. Burney.

Fordham, July 10, 1774

I mentioned some traces of temperament in the
Greek writers. Had the ancients a temperament?
taking the word in its most general sense, for an
alteration of intervals from their strict ratio, or tune,
they most certainly had.

Aristoxenus is fairly enough called by the Abbé
Roussier *chef des températeurs.* For his great first
principle—*i e.* that the ear is the sole judge—is the
very principle of a temperament which is founded
upon the imperfection of the ear, or its latitude in admitting sounds for the same, which are not exactly so

Could one speak in strange terms of our modern
bouleversement of tuning? And the sanctum sanc-
torum invaded too! the *soni immobiles,* the great distance posts of the system, that were driven down into
the centre of the earth, torn up! the great beacons and
lighthouses of the tetrachords pulled down, and the
ear left afloat, without any guide, in the midst of all
the flats, and shoals, and breakers of the modes,
genera, colours, divisions and sub-divisions of this un-
pacific ocean! For Plutarch adds, ' Tuning flat not

only the moveable sounds, but even some of the immoveable.'

It is not easy to understand exactly how all this was   What was their view? why all was flattened in this manner ? But it is very plain that the musicians of that time were all for Wilkes and liberty in their tuning. Ἔκλυσις and ἐκβολή! No ; may I be laid all the rest of my life upon the rack of the Greek diagram, stretched out till my head touch Nete and my toes Proslambanomenos ; like St. Lawrence upon his gridiron, with all the crossbars of the scale flaying my poor back, and the vulture of curiosity gnawing my liver all the while, if I utter a word about them !

The dramatic music of the ancients I never thought much about, and the little that I saw without thinking always appeared very strange to me. If one may judge (and why not ?) of this part of their theatrical exhibitions by the others—by their decorations, dresses, &c., and by their drama itself, it must have been a very simple, rude kind of a thing. Their tragedies, which the prejudiced admirers of the ancients talk about as perfect, finished models, are nothing like it. They are the rude, imperfect sketches of men of genius ; sometimes sublime, sometimes mean and vulgar to the last degree ; and, perhaps in the same page, sometimes highly poetical, sometimes worse than prosaic , with fine strokes of nature and manifest absurdities side by side But, as d'Alembert says admirably : ' On s'est donné bien de la peine

pour étudier une langue difficile ; on ne peut pas
avoir perdu son temps ; on veut même paroître aux
yeux des autres récompensé avec usure des peines
qu'on a prises ; et on leur dit avec un froid transport ·
" Ah ! si vous sçaviez le Grec ! "' And what are we
to think of their masks, their stilts, their mouthpieces,
their stuffed dresses, and all the other parts of the same
gigantic theatrical system ? Diderot asserts that poetry
was introduced upon the Greek stage as a necessary
part of the same plan , *i e.* to make the actors more
distinctly heard and understood in their immense
theatres, crowded with a noisy multitude. It appears
to me that music was introduced by the same necessity It was not enough to declaim their poetry ;
they were to sing it, or rather to chant it, in order to
be heard. It was plainly impossible the actors should
be heard in all parts of such vast open theatres without raising the voice far higher than its natural pitch ;
to speak so is shocking to the ear, therefore they
sung. How the accompaniment answered this end
I don't see , but it added to the noise, and to the
musical entertainment of the audience, and was some
soulagement to the actors, and saved their lungs and
their mouthpieces. The notion of Rousseau, Abbé du
Bos, and others, that the ancients had a noted declamation, and that their language was so accented and
melodious as to be capable of musical accompaniment,
without ceasing to be speech—I am not the most
positive of human beings, but if this is not rank non-

sense I give up my understanding. No doubt some
languages are more musical than others—the Italian,
for instance, than the French ; and the Greek may
have been as far beyond the Italian. But that any
language, even its most musical form—that of declamation—should differ so widely from all others we
know of as to want the characteristic difference that
separates all speech from song, *i.e.* the continued
motion up and down (*per gradus*, and not *per saltum*),
is absolutely incredible. And while that essential
difference subsisted, it certainly could not be accompanied by instruments. Rousseau says . ' It is impossible to understand what the ancients have said of
their theatrical declamation without supposing this.'
I don't quite see that, but be it so ; is not it better to
say at once that we do not understand them, than to
explain them into impossibilities ? The Abbé du
Bos was all over system in history, music, and what
not. No man proves his point more resolutely ; he
wields all sorts of authors to his purpose, and trans-
lates them as he pleases. But here is the rock I set
my foot upon. It seems certain that the ancient
drama was accompanied by musical instruments ;
I conclude confidently, that since the instruments
could not speak, the actors must sing ; their declamation must certainly have been, strictly speaking, musical, however simple ; for the chanting of
the simplest plain chant is as truly and essentially
music as the most refined melody of a modern opera.

I suppose the dialogue was a chanting sort of recitative, and the monologues, or cantica, answered to our airs. I can't conceive the accompaniment to have been in harmony, like ours, because the utmost use of harmony that I can find any proof of among the ancients amounts to no more than the flinging in a chord now and then, or a little sprinkling of arpeggio, or somewhat like what our old musicians called breaking a ground. The striking a note now and then, like our recitatives, is a modern idea ; and being arbitrary and not founded, that I see, upon any natural necessity, is not, I think, to be hastily applied to those ancient operas.

The steps by which ancient music got forward into modern, and melody slid by degrees into harmony, I take to be one of the darkest processes of the dark ages. I have long observed that almost every kind of noise produced by hitting one kind of thing against another, hard or soft, has in it somewhat to my ear of musical pitch, some sound effect of high and low. I find Isaac Vossius had this fancy ; great authority, sir ! Nay, he appeals to all the musical world : 'Norunt omnes musicæ periti, nullum posse fingi sonum, qui concentui aptari non possit.' If noise differs from musical sound—to begin philosophising about sound will never do—I'm glad I stopped myself in time. . . . By the by, what miserable hobbling stuff are the smooth airs, as Milton calls them, of Henry Lawes ? Purcell, with all his old curls and twiddles, is perfection to him.

It is not a journey that I fear in summer, but a journey to London, and being there in summer. Here we shall be quite snug ; I have seldom visitors, and no neighbours. Except that I am married, I live the life of a hermit, and my beard is sometimes as long as a hermit's—one of the greatest blessings of a country life, where

> All the night in silver sleep I spend,
> All the day long to what I list attend.

A GOSSIPING LETTER.—PERCY'S 'RELIQUES.'—CHAU-
CER'S TALES.—BURNEY'S 'HISTORY OF MUSIC.'

To Dr. Burney.

Colchester, Jan. 27, 1776.

There is something so solemn and frightful in this long silence that I can endure it no longer ; I should not have had patience so long if I had not been afraid of our letters meeting and jostling one another upon the road, for do you know I have had the assurance to expect to hear from you every day for this fort-night past ? But I can give no other reason than that I wished it ; for I acknowledge with all humility that my last *barbouillage* was a sneaking return for your amusing *étrennes* — '*marqué au coin de l'ai-mable folie.*' Pooh ! as if you stood upon that cere-mony ! Pray abuse me—but I remember slumping all on a sudden into the slough of despond, and clos-ing my letter in the dumps. I meet with these acci-dents now and then, but, thank God, I soon work myself out again.   Chiaroscuro, pianofoite, light and shade, contrast, hill and dale, winter and summer—'tis all very well and very pretty.   And so let us talk of fifty different things in a minute.   I long to know how you do, and what ?   Mr. Wegg and I begin now to look out for your book.   Ha! well! whereabouts have you whipt in all your straggling dogs of scrips ? when do you present ?   When do you ?—I'm out of breath. . . .   Really that is an elegant, valuable publication of Percy's.[1]   Many of those old songs, I confess, are to me beautiful and touching ; and many others diverting and curious.   Do you know 'Balow my Babe' (vol. ii p. 196)?   'Tis touching to me, and sweet, I declare ; somewhat similar in subject to the 'Danae' of Simonides, but how far beyond it ?   Oh! this puts me in mind of some two or three lines you once repeated to me from an old Scotch travesty of the Bible—'What have we here?' &c.   I beseech you down with them in your next letter, for they are admirable, and I have often wanted to recal them. Here's another Simonidean 'Madonna col bambino' from Chaucer (Man of Lawe's Tale) :—

> Hire littel child lay weeping in hire arm,
> And kneeling piteously to him she said,
> ' Peace, littel son, I wot do thee no harm.'

---

[1] Note by Richard Twining, the nephew of Thomas Twining, 1853 .—' Percy's *Reliques*.   Well do I remember the evenings at Isleworth, when after supper we formed a wide circle round the fire, my father often reading some of these olden rhymes to my mother and ourselves.   " Visions of the past, I greet ye still."'—R. T.

> With that, hire coverchief of hire head she braid,
> And over his littel eyen she it laid ;
> And in hire arms she lulleth it full fast,
> And into the heven hire eyen up she cast.

Mrs. B. has been a reader of Chaucer ; I desire to know whether she does not think this picture charming. There is a fine stroke afterwards. Addressing the Virgin, she says—

> Thou saw thy child yslain before thine eyen,
> And yet now liveth my littel child, parfay !

Don't you like that ?

I have *entamé* the memoirs of Petrarch, and find them delightful miscellaneous reading. Do you know who is the author ? I was always a great admirer of the natural and genuine part of Petrarch's poetry. But I relish his sonnets and canzoni still more when I read them in the memories introduced with all the circumstances that can help to explain them, and to make the subject interesting. The first thing I looked at in your dedication[1] was what you said of me—*c'est la nature.*[2] I held up my fan, and looked through the sticks, as Fielding's squeamish lady did. It really looks very well, and is a very pretty, fat, light, sleek, compact little *éloge* ; but it holds a monstrous deal, and I wish it was as near the truth in my mind as perhaps it may be in yours. But I, who know the man, can only shake my head as I bow it.

[1] Referring to Burney's *History of Music*, of which the first volume was published in 1776.

[2] He was mentioned in the Preface.

D

NOTES OF AN ENGLISH TOUR MADE IN 1776.

Written to his Brother.

Did you ever form a plan that you kept strictly to upon your journey ? It seems to me but lost labour to determine so exactly where we shall dine, or sleep, beforehand ; these things are best left to settle themselves as you go. We did not follow any one of our plans. We slept at Huntingdon as we proposed, and got to Stamford by dinner the next day, intending to see Burleigh in the afternoon ; but the rain and the distracting bustle of the George Inn, which exceeded anything I ever saw or heard, determined us to give up Burleigh till our return, and go to Colsterworth, where we lay ; and a snug comfortable dormitory it is. The evening was wet and unpleasant, yet I could not help paddling round the village, and pleasing myself with the thought that Master Isaac Newton had often done the same thing at the time when he used to skulk about with a book of mathematics in his pocket, and hide himself in hay lofts to work problems. I told you I was pleased with a little valley on the right, about two miles beyond Colsterworth ; a gentleman's house, and a village (I believe Easton) well embosomed in trees. (The place you thought Kingford must be Water Newton, from whence you look down upon the Nene and its meadows.)

Grantham is rather a pretty town altogether, but the spire struck me prodigiously. My eyes are neither compasses, rulers, nor quadrants ; but it appeared to me the highest I had ever seen, and it is beautifully preserved ; all the ornaments and lace work are fresh upon it ; one would think it was kept in a shagreen case like an urn or a coffee-pot, and only uncovered on Sunday to see company. One comes upon it very advantageously. It peeps like the point of a needle over the hill, rises higher and higher as you advance, you think the spire has no bottom. At last the tower peeps and rises in the same manner till you reach the top of the hill.

It has a fine effect. Expectation and gradual discovery make it still higher than it really is. Then it has such a Parmigiano slimness ! As well as I can remember, it is much beyond Salisbury spire. If the spire of Grantham church was taken off, it seems to me that the tower alone would be uncommonly high. But I know how much I may be deceived in all this comparative estimation.

From Hoocliff Hill, about two miles beyond Grantham, you have a view somewhat sublime and striking from its mere extent and suddenness ; but it is flat as a pancake. I admired it as I went, and said nothing about it as I came back. The road is through level, moorish, unpleasant ground from the bottom of that hill to Newark, but, as road, excellent. Newark is neat and handsome, well-paved, clean,

many good houses, and a large market-place, which
will be nobly decorated by the building now carrying
on—a mayor's house of stone, with a front that I
thought good architecture, with portico and pediment.

The church is large and handsome ; but the spire
looks clumsy after Grantham, though the next best
that I saw. The old ruined castle is very large, and
a great ornament to the north entrance—Slept at
Tuxford, two miles beyond Scarthen Moor, for
the sake of getting on a little further. Nothing
worth notice.—Sunday morning, breakfasted at
the ' Bell,' Barnby Moor, a gentleman-like, comfortable house. (It may be useful to you to know
that in your future travels) Dined and slept at
Doncaster. From Barnby to Doncaster the face of
things improves, and the glories of Yorkshire begin to
be announced : fine, open, bold views, though poor
in comparison of what we saw when we quitted the
great road and turned to the left towards Barnsley.
Bawtry (I should have said sooner) is a very clean,
cheerful-looking town, and makes no unhandsome
doorcase to the county It is only one unpaved
street, and appears only as a larger sort of village,
though a market-town. The approach to Doncaster,
through rows of high trees on each side of a wide
road, is promising, and the appearance of the High
Street, at the first entrance, handsome. But I am
tired of using these general words, that convey no

ideas. To be sure, now, you have a very distinct idea of Doncaster from my calling it handsome! That which principally gives the street its nobility is the mayor's house, which you see—among other good-looking buildings—as soon as you enter it, at some distance on the left. (I don't mean out of the street, but some way before you.) It is a stone building, with portico, pediment, &c., but by no means so elegant as the building at Newark. It is heavy and fine, the entrance bothered with a cluster of pillars on each side that are crowded close together, and seem to have no business there—they look as if they had run thither from their stations in other parts of the buildings to stand and see the company come in ; for the assembly-room is there, and if it had not been Sunday I would have seen it, for it is talked much of. When I talk of a ‘ cluster ’ of pillars, I may misrepresent without intending it : it is too multitudinous a word. I think there are at least three or four pillars on each side, and, I believe, not room for a man to stand between them. How soon these things grow bleared and blotty in one's memory! If it was of any importance I should blame myself for not having *journalised* a little more particularly on the spot. When I go into Italy I will be less lazy. In every respect but that of the market-place I think Doncaster a better town than Newark.

Monday morning we set off for Barnsley, and found the road so rough, and bad, and tedious (our wheels too wide for the ruts) that we were too much out of humour to observe how pleasant it was. Soon after we turned off, we passed a good house, finely situated, which I found belonged to Godfrey Went-worth, an old customer and acquaintance of my father's with whom we used whilom to fiddle. Elm-sall met us a little on this side Barnsley, where we *broke* fast. (Break, broke—why not breakfast, *broke-fast*?) You know Barnsley, and that it is not called black for nothing. From thence to Emley the country is truly charming; but description is impossible, and you have seen some of it, and know the style.

After a few days' rest at Emley, our first expe-dition was a walk to Denby, a little village about three miles off, to dine with a brother of Mr. Elmsall's, whose house is in the most beautiful situation of the snug sort I ever saw—somewhat similar to my neigh-bour Boys's, but upon a larger scale, and far more striking. You would have laughed to have seen Elmsall leading me with my eyes shut into the garden, that I might open them upon the spot where I might enjoy the whole effect at once. The ground descends from the house, and then rises in a very high hill, covered with a beautiful hanging wood to the very top, exceedingly steep, and all near the eye. Sir John Kay's old mansion is perched on the right, and appears above the wood, and a neat farmhouse or two on the left of it, opposite to you. The wood extends a considerable way to the left; but on that

side the valley opens, and you have a catch of beautiful distant view, which forms a fine contrast to the
other, and heightens the calmness and repose of the
situation, by giving one a peep of the world that one
seems to have left. There wants nothing but water
to make the spot completely beautiful. The house is
a very good one—land with it ; the rent very reasonable, Mr. Elmsall going to quit it ; if I had had no
friends, no local ties, I verily believe I should have
taken it. If ever you turn hermit, think of Denby.
We were detained by rain all night. It is all the same,
I find, to the good people in Yorkshire whether you
stay an hour or a month with them ; they are never
incommoded. I envy them the style of easy hospitality they live in, still more than their prospects or
their coals.

The next morning we walked to Whitley, to see a
noble extensive view from Mr. Beaumont's temple, a
large summer-house at the end of a long terrace.
Here I was made to look through a telescope, and to
see York Minster whether I would or no When I
find people resolutely determined that I shall see a
thing, I always see it immediately, to save trouble.
From hence we walked to Emley to dinner. I believe
our walk that morning was not less than eight
miles.

Our next excursion was to Sandall Castle Hill,
near Wakefield. You may read about it in Hume's
' History ' (vol. ii., year 1460)—how the Duke of York

threw himself into Sandall Castle, and, like a fool, threw himself out again, to be killed in the battle of Wakefield. Don't imagine this was all our reason for going to this hill, or indeed any part of it. It commands a beautiful view of Wakefield, the Calder, and all the adjacent country, which is rich, cultivated, wooded, watered, enclosed, inhabited, what not? It was the best view I had yet seen of the large kind. Wakefield has a peculiarly clean and cheerful appearance at a distance as well as near ; the buildings look fresh and new ; I believe they wash their roofs and chimneys there. The hill is high, round, small, and its ascent almost perpendicular, a little fragment of the castle still standing. The place is wild, venerable, and covered with old trees, which on every side set off the view by interrupting it. You see the Calder glittering through the boughs.

We dined at Kettlethorpe, just by, with some hospitable friends of Mr Elmsall's ; but before dinner we walked about half a mile, and saw a piece of water of Sir Lionel Pilkington's, that pleased me much ; it is surrounded with hanging woods to its edge, and is in miniature what I conceive some of the Westmoreland lakes to be ; but it was not the only object—you see with it the village of Kettlethorpe scattered here and there upon broken romantic ground—houses, cottages, craggy hills, climbing pathways, road, water, wood, well mixed and beautiful. Oh ! this green trencher of a county called Essex ! where we think it

a sublime thing to look over one hedge and see
another. Well, thank God it is not Lincolnshire,
Cambridgeshire, nor Huntingdonshire. My glass [1]
answered charmingly upon this spot

The next meal my eyes made was in Sir Thomas
Wentworth's wood at Bretton Hall, within an evening's walk of Emley. There is no end of description
conceive a large wood upon the side of a hill, cut out
into walks, with vistas and little openings that show
you from time to time bright catches of distant views,
made more distinct and beautiful by being, as it were,
set in a frame of shade ; a large water beneath, which
you come down to by degrees, after seeing here and
there a little peep of it glimmering through the plan-
tation of firs, &c. The water is long and wide, and
has the appearance of a considerable river, wooded on
each side, an island with a building on it, boats, &c.
I did think it a little hard, as I walked along, that I
could not have such a place to live at as well as Sir
T. Wentworth. A pleasant kind of grumbling, that
might find one employment for one's whole life.

Next in my little journalet stands our expedition
to Ealand, or (as pronounced) Elland. It is twelve
miles from Emley, and we went to dine there upon
one of the hottest days I ever felt, merely to see the
view and return. Though, indeed, it is a view everywhere ; for I never had so pleasant a ride in my life ;
we went one way and returned another, both roads an

[1] Gray's Mirror.

uninterrupted series of beautiful prospects. I can
safely say that we passed over no indifferent spot.
We went by Whitley, and the greatest beauty on that
road is the view of Kirklees, Sir George Armitage's,
with which I was enchanted ; a rich valley, water,
bridges, hills, and woods, &c. It was the best
thing I had seen yet on account of the water ; less
extensive than other views, but more distinct, near,
and picturesque. You descend to Elland by a hill
monstrously long, and very steep, which we walked
down. The view from this hill was the finest I had
seen of the extensive kind, the Calder winding through
the meadows below the town, high hills covered with
thicker, closer, and larger woods than I saw anywhere
else.

I thought this was all I had to see, and that
nothing would do after it. After we had put up our
horses, and ordered dinner at Elland, we walked
through the town, which is dirty, and promises nothing,
to the turnpike at one end of it (I forget whither the
road leads), where you come suddenly upon the view
I told you of, and which is far beyond anything that
my scanty travels have ever shown me. You see
partly the same objects which you saw from the hill
above the town ; but everything is nearer, more distinct, compact, and picturesque ; and the great beauty
of all (and which I think essential to a first-rate view)
is, that you look down directly upon it, and it begins
from the feet of the spectator ; a circumstance totally

out of the reach of painting, and only to be found in
God's landscapes! You stand upon the road ; over
your head are high cliffs, on the top of which is a foot-
path ; directly under you another road; under that,
the river winding along through green meadows, with
a fall or two that have more effect to the ear than to
the eye ; to the right, on the side you stand on, the
church and town hanging upon the hill, with cottages,
&c., quite down to the water's side ; the bridge, beyond it the river losing itself among woody hills, the
valley opening to a distant view, where you catch a
last glimmer of the river before it finally departs. To
the left the river, after a long winding, loses itself
(nearer to the eye) by turning to the right among high
hills richly covered with woods, the rock in some
places peeping through them. These woods extend
on the opposite side of the river both ways as far as
you can see, only a beautiful green rim of meadow
between them and the river. Immediately under the
wood is a path that accompanies the river as far as
you can see to the left, and must be the most delicious
of all walks. Imagine all the living accompaniments
to this scene ; cattle feeding in the meadows, boys
bathing, people on foot and horseback, above, below,
over your head, and under your feet. After dining in
a charming cellar-like room at the Savile Arms (the
whole place and all its environs are Sir George
Savile's), made on purpose to cool heated travellers,
we had a mind to see the view again from the highest

path, which was over our heads ; but, fine as it was,
we agreed that the road below was the best spot ;
above the view becomes more distant, greater, but less
beautiful and piquant. We could discover Halifax
from this height ; indeed, it is but a few miles from
Elland ; the valley through which the river winds to
your left hand leads to it, and is all in the same
beautiful style. And so, farewell Elland ; if I forget
thee, let my right hand forget her cunning ! We returned by Huddersfield ; more and steeper hills, but
the whole way if possible more beautiful than the
other, though in rather a different style.

The next day (by a silly engagement that I shall
always lament, because it hindered our going on from
Elland to Halifax through the vale of delights) we
dined at ——— with a fine, florid, curtseying old
lady, that gets a heap of musical people together now
and then ; gives them exceeding good dinners of
savoury meat such as their souls love ; jams them all
up in a little basking summer-house by way of fresco
and coolness, begs a song of this Miss, a lesson of
that, and the favour of a concerto or a trio ; and
curtsies and thanks, and is vastly obliged, and then
lets them all go, and thinks she has had a concert.
We supped very pleasantly with Mr. Elmsall's mother ;
you must know I am passionately fond of agreeable
old women ; not those that are still young in airs and
vanity, like Mrs. ———, but in spirits, sense, and good
humour. I think I could do no greater favour to a

young woman than to make her, if I had it in my power, like two or three old ones that I know, in every respect but person. My journal grows enormous; 'tis time to get on a little. The next day we were to dine at Thornhill, which obliged us to walk to Heath before breakfast, or we should not have seen it. Of all walks near a town that I ever saw, 'tis the pleasantest, but you have been at Wakefield and Heath, therefore description is needless. We went to Thornhill by Dewsbury Bank, where you come upon a view which, I think, stands first in my list of views upon the great scale; your sister was more struck with it than even with the Vale of Elland. As for describing it, it would be like describing the world. It is such a map! We dined and lay at Thornhill, at the house of a brother-in-law of Mr. E, where we were most comfortably entertained with all the essentials of politeness, without its bows and grimaces. We found we were welcome, but were not told it. Thornhill stands very singularly, near the top of a bank, about two miles long, which is called Thornhill Edge; the width of the level top is not above two common sized fields, so that the place is surrounded by very extensive and fine prospects; yet in itself snug and comfortable. The descent of the bank is on both sides very steep and abrupt, we walked in the evening round the edge, in a narrow path between the hedge and the hill, which in some places is almost perpendicular. We saw

chimneys smoking directly under us, and were shocked
to see little children playing fearlessly upon the very
brink of the precipice. The next morning after
breakfast we walked, sweltered with heat, to a hill
between Thornhill and Denby to see another view,
which, had I seen it sooner, would have astonished
me. Upon the whole, Dewsbury Bank is more cheerful, and has more distinctness about it. We walked
on to Denby, dined there, and had our horses brought
to meet us, and drank tea at Emley, well fatigued
with the labours of four sultry days ; bothered, burnt,
and stupid, and glad by way of variety to sit quietly
down and see nothing. Accordingly we saw no more
till we left Emley.

Friday, August 9.—Broke fast at Bank Top, from
whence we had the view of Lord Stafford's, which you
have seen. There cannot well be a finer country than
that between Bank Top and Sheffield, where we dined
and slept ; but unluckily it rained hard almost all the
way, and the head of the chaise deprived us of all side
view. The parts that struck me most were to the
north of Ecclesfield and Sheffield. But it was the
torment of Tantalus. The rain continued almost all
the afternoon and evening, and prevented our leaving
the inn in time enough to see anything of the manu-
factures, though we did get a pleasant little walk up to
our knees, through the Peacroft into 'Sootland.' I never
saw so black a place ; but you have been there. Next
day we had a terrible eighteen miles to go to Worksop

before breakfast; the pavement of Sheffield, which you
know is execrable, reaches almost two miles from the
town; after that, for a mile or two, it was so cut up and
bad as to be hardly safe; and from thence, to within
about four miles of Worksop, it is all rugged and jumb-
ling, much worse than a tolerably good pavement. We
were so tired, sick, and discouraged when we got to
Worksop, that we had not spirits to think of going an
inch out of our way, and so gave up our intention of
going through the parks, because we found it was four
miles about, and required a guide. We afterwards re-
pented, when we found the common road flat and
stupid, and no traces of all the magnificence and
finery which we knew lay hid in the woods a little
way on our right hand. But to say the truth, the
great scenes of nature that I had been seeing left me
very indifferent about houses and parks, and even in
a great measure about pictures. Worksop is very
neat and gentlemanlike, and a complete contrast to
Sheffield; but Nottinghamshire seems to have few
natural beauties. It is nine miles to Ollerton; we
wished to go farther before dinner, and so we pushed
on to a little place called Knesall, in the Duke of
Kingston's dominions, where we were forced to dine
upon bread and cheese and butter and cucumber,
which was no punishment to me. The Worksop
people had told us we might dine there. Slept at
Newark. Next day (Sunday) breakfast at ———,
intending to go to church, and set out immediately

after; but Poppet[1] was taken ill, and detained us there till Monday morning.

I am determined to keep within the bounds of this fourth sheet, and so I must be swift and sententious Monday, dined and slept at Stamford, and saw Burleigh; we talked of the pictures, and my memorandums about them are short, few, and not worth communicating. I saw them in haste, and cloudy weather; I scarce saw them at all. I shall be glad when I have your journal to see whether the same things struck us both. Pray let me have it; it would entertain me more now than at another time I have not the courage to read over this long scrawl, which I have got through by fits and snatches. I have often said it is the height of folly to attempt to describe views; yet I could not help trying, and you know you are not to say to your brother, thou fool! One thing more · I caution you against the misrepresentations, exaggerations, amplifications, colourings of fancy, mistakes of memory, and lies of all sorts which may be, and I dare say are, in this account of mine. Not that I had the least intention to deceive you, or know where I have done it. But it is a certain truth that people of imagination and strong feelings never describe fairly. 'Let no such man be trusted.' If the reader is of the same stamp, it is still worse; there will be two imaginations conspiring against poor naked truth; one in relating, the other

[1] 'Poppet'—his horse.

in understanding. Therefore if you are ever likely to see anything I have described, forget all this, or make large deductions if you would not be certainly disappointed. To-morrow (Monday, September 9) we go to Skreens for the week ; not to Mr. Natts, as we were to have done.

CHATTERTON'S POEMS.

To his Brother.

April, 1777.

I read the Rowley poems[1] through after you left me, and found them full of genius. There are touches here and there that Mr. Gray would not have been ashamed of. The tragic interlude of Ælla is fine almost all through. In short, the book I think is full of uncommon beauties ; and I have settled it in my mind that it is partly forged, and partly not. There are many things which it is in the highest degree improbable that Chatterton should have thought of. He must have found some old fragments, at least, which led and assisted his invention, gave him ideas, and put him in the way. Lines left out, or illegible, he supplied, and rough ones, I suppose, he polished and harmonised. Mr. Forster has read the book, and is of my opinion. I assure you I can scarce bear any poetry that I have taken up after it. What think

------

[1] Probably in the edition published by Tyrwhitt in 1777. Chatterton died in August 1770.

E

you of this image of a discontented, murmuring, re-
monstrating people ?

> . . . 'to the king
> They roll their troubles like a surgy sea !'

THE FASCINATIONS OF READING. — DR BURNEY'S
'HISTORY OF MUSIC.'—'ROWLEY' AND CHATTER-
TON.—AN OLD PSALM TUNE

To Dr. Burney

Fordham, June 16, 1777

You desired me to write 'before hot weather
lollops came on,' and so I do Can you complain ?
And yet I hope you can and do ; at least I do, of
myself and my idleness. It is just as you say ; one
is often violently industrious one way and violently
idle another at the same time. I have been reading
like a dragon, if that will be any comfort to you. I
wish I could leave off this silly trick. I have sometimes a great mind to administer an oath to myself
that I will read nothing for one whole year, by way
of experiment. I wonder what would be the effect ?
Sometimes I think I should find myself very much
improved at the year's end , sometimes I think I
should hang myself, *par ennui* ; sometimes I think
it would work a great metamorphosis upon me—all
outdoor-ness and bodily activity, with a fat lump of
quiet mind within ; the very image of a man asleep
in a post-chaise ; a brisk, noisy, back-slapping new

man, with a round hat and a skirtless coat, with
gunpowder pockets under his armpits ready for the
partridges in September (Do you like me so ?) But
sometimes I think the only consequence would be
that the stream of literary habit, stopped one way
would find out another, and, through the narrow
ducts and strainers of the brain, work itself out into
books and pamphlets. Well, but now we talk oi
books.

   .   .   .   .   .   .

Oh ! but now I must scold you a little. Why
you really talk about your *opus magnum* in a very
cavalier way, as if you did not care a farthing
whether you ever finished it or not ! I tell you
plainly, I shall not suffer this. Why, pray now, what
is the matter ? What are you afraid of ? (The lamb
giving the lion a lecture upon courage : smoke him !)
Is not the worst half of your labour over ? and have
you not got with great credit through the most un-
popular, unpromising, and dry part of it ? What the
deuce, then, should make you shrink now, when
almost all drudgery, and gropery, and pokery is
over ; when you have plenty of materials to produce,
and every step will bring you into a more pleasurable
country, where you may have recourse to your own
ideas and taste, which no man can have filched from
you, and where you will be original, &c. ? Pray,
good Mr. Laziness, think of this, and jump up, and
rub your hands, and give your breeches a hitch up

E 2

and show a little life and spirit—look at *me !* But really, now, don't be such a renegade ; but when you get into your summer quarters do a little something, in a cool, comfortable way, and don't stay till the devil drives you.

Now I am down upon my knees again, to you and good Mrs. B., to beg pardon for the trouble I give you in hunting and shaking Exumeno and Petrarch for *mes chétifs papiers.* I made a mistake. I should have desired you to search for my memory —for that was all I had lost—not my papers, which I found in my bureau here, at Fordham, at my return, where they had slept safely all the winter, though if you had desired me to send you an affidavit of their removal with me to Colchester, I should certainly have done it without scruple or hesitation. Ay! ay! I hear you all laughing me to scorn. I expected it, and deserve it. What hunts had I ! When I saw them in my bureau, I thought of nothing but the monkey postillion that ran away from the man with his dog-chaise some years ago : do you remember ? The man hunted for him half over the town, and at last, when he came back to his chaise, sweating and cursing, and vowing vengeance, there sate the monkey in his place, waiting for his master, with as much coolness and *sang froid* as if nothing had happened.

.   .   .   .   .   .

Can you tell me, *par hasard*, what Mr. Mason

thinks of Rowley's poems ? Whatever he may think of their authenticity, if he did not allow them to be full of genius I should scarce be able to think him sincere. What a fuss people make whether Rowley or Chatterton wrote them, as if the whole merit of the poetry depended upon that point ! Nothing will do but a rarity ; but I know of no greater rarity than such genius as appears in those poems. Aye, but the precious mould and the cobwebs! For my part, I have made up, long ago, my creed about these things. I believe that they are neither all old nor all modern ; that Chatterton found some MSS, deciphered where he could, supplied where he could not, here and there embellished and polished, perhaps ; that he was himself a lad of genius, and able to catch a spirit, and imitate tolerably what he could never have entirely invented.

How go you and yours ? and do you move towards Lynn this summer ? for the case is, my brother and I talk of a trip to Houghton [1] about the middle of next month ; now to meet you there would be—— No ! stay, it won't do. I shall be talking to you instead of looking at the pictures. I desire no such company. But you may tell me if I have any chance of such a mishap. I have another chance of a peep at some of you sweet creatures. We talk of a visit to Twit'nam this summer ; so I shall just call to see who takes care of your house in St.

---

[1] They did go, and saw that noble gallery in the best way—left to themselves.

Martin's Street.   If I am so unlucky as to find none
of you there, I will beg of the servant just to let me
sit and sigh half an hour in the parlour till

Con molto pensiero indi mi svello !

Mind and lock up your music ; for I fear I should
go upstairs and rummage your skeleton case, and
steal all the Emanuel Bach's [1] I can find, in revenge for
your not helping me, as you said you would (if I had
patience, and I have had patience above this twelve-
month), to complete my collection.   Mrs. B. played
me one of a set I never saw before, and I have panted
after it ever since.

Here is a most curious piece of barbarism for you.
This psalm-tune is often sung at Colchester.   It may
have a name, and be nothing new to you ; but I never
heard anything so horrible and strange ; 'tis worse
than a Greek fragment :—

Selah [1]

Il faut finir !   Pray forgive me and write soon ;
for I think this same silence is but a melancholy
thing.   Remember me to Mrs. B. and the whole
witchery.

[1] Sebastian Bach, the composer of the Passion Music, was the
elder brother.   Probably Emanuel Bach's music may have been at that
time the greater novelty, and so have attracted the special attention of
the correspondents.

INTERCHANGE OF CRITICISMS. — A GOOD-NATURED
MAN.—PLANS FOR THE FUTURE.

To his Brother.

Fordham, November 6, 1778.

I hope Pliny, and your copy-book, and my copy-
book will get safe to you in this packet I give you
a week to find where my MS. begins. I wish that
trouble, and the trouble of deciphering an execrable
hand, pejorated by hurrying to save time, and crowd-
ing to save room, may answer to you. I wanted to
have got all into the book ; but was forced at last to
tack on an appendix. I believe all monsters have
tails. You may possibly think my remarks sometimes dry and sometimes trifling ; for sometimes
they dissert about words, and sometimes explain
constructions, joinings, &c., which very likely you
may not want to have explained. But I was aware
that the best taste and discernment will not secure
a reader young in a language from now and then
taking things wrong. Indeed, the more taste and
feeling a man has the more irksome it is to him to
suspend them, as it were, in order to attend to
grammar, syntax, and derivation ; so that this part
of my MS. I hold to be more to your purpose than
any other. Matters of taste, or general criticism, I
have entered into only to please myself by talking
to you and comparing notes with you. Nothing of
this sort do you want. I hope to see your remarks

upon the remainder of this book where I have gone on without you. I thought it was better to finish at once   Pray go on with your conversation in the 8th book, &c., &c.   I shall go on with my replies ; but I must devise some decent bounds for my loquacity, if only that you may have no scruples.   Nay, you need have none ; for had I confined myself to answer your remarks I should not have been so voluminous.   Don't think yourself obliged to say something to all I have said.   I leave you entirely at liberty ; only don't be silent to spare me, for your communications of this, and indeed of every sort, are one of the pleasantest ingredients in the seasoning of my life.

Now, let me just look for a few odds and ends unanswered in your last letter. I think the only fault Hey has in writing is that his expression is not always so clear as his ideas   I have often told him so, now and formerly.   But he writes in general exceedingly well, and, what is best of all in him, he writes from himself and his own notions, without echoing anybody, yet with a candour and fairness uncommon in all writers.

'Why am I always correcting the MSS. of others ? '—Because, sir, I am a mighty good-natured, obliging sort of a fellow, and always ready to lend my friends my spectacles, such as they are ; and then I am not so very good-humoured but that I have a very pretty gift of faultfinding.   'Why do I write nothing myself?'—Why, I do intend, if I live and do well (though I believe I shall not do well in that case), to write fifty things; the first of which will be a translation of Aristotle's Poetics,[1] with notes that will be a treasure of erudition, taste, criticism, &c., &c.! But you need not advertise this yet. Then my 35th book of Pliny, my musical treatise, &c., you'll see— you'll see—one of these days. The worst of it is, I have so many things to read that I have no time to write. As to your reading prose between whiles, it would be very well if you had the leisure I have; but even I (and I think we settled that point here in my garden) always find, when I attempt to read two books together, that one swallows up the other, unless the subordinate, under-plot book be very light and easy reading. You must be some time in getting through your present undertaking; and as you return to it only at intervals, and never, I imagine, for very long together, you stand the less in need of relief from variety. Heyne's prose is ten times harder than any you will find in Cicero. The reading his notes must be considered as good, useful, rough prose exercise.

[1] This, I am happy to say, he did accomplish, and I have heard him speak seriously of Pliny. The trouble that *Aristotle* gave him, and the declining state of his health, prevented his undertaking any other work.—R. T., 1818.

After his death the whole of the quarto edition of his *Aristotle* was sold, and a second edition in 8vo was published by his nephew and literary executor, the Rev. Daniel Twining, late Rector of Therfield.— R. T., 1881.

We are setting our faces towards Colchester. Thursday I rode to Notley to dine with some four-and-twenty farmers, for which I made them pay me 100*l.*, and rode home with it yesterday in my pocket. It was fairly worth the money.

ORIGINAL IDEAS ABOUT WALES. — VISIT TO A FRIEND'S PARSONAGE.—LITERARY PURSUITS.

To his Brother.

Fordham, July 29, 1779.

I trembled lest I should be too late for my word. I promised to write to you while in Wales, and I hope to do so ; but upon consulting my almanac, and calculating, I find I have stayed longer than I meant to have done. However, I will hope that I may still catch you upon some Welsh mountain, or in some village of Ll's, and ww's, and dd's, that will hereafter be seen, but not read, in the journal of your tour. And how do you both do ? and where are you, have you been, and shall you be ? I should have said all three, for I recollect hearing that Richard was of your party. Have you been civil to the goats, and drank plentifully of their milk ? I hope you have, for I think I have heard it reckoned the most fattening and restoring of all potations. Mrs. Burney went into Wales a year or two ago on purpose, I think, to drink goat's milk, and received great benefit. I have an idea of your lying upon your back upon the side of a mountain, and

sucking a she-goat that you have caught by the leg as
it frisked about you.   I desire you may return home
with your body full of rich blood, and your head full
of rich ideas.   I shall long to hear some account of
you, and yet I will not have you hurry yourself to
write.   My idea of Wales (it must needs be diverting
to a man who is in Wales) is that there are nowhere
two inches of plain ground in it ; that you keep bobbing
up and down as you go, into the clouds and out of
them again ; that the bottom of the lowest valley is
at least as high as Danbury, the highest ground in
Essex ; that it is very troublesome travelling to a
man of any humanity, from the continual danger of
running over goats, and from the impossibility of
asking the way to any place, though you knew the
name of it ; that the Welsh are a very good sort of
hospitable, good-natured people, every man believing
himself descended from King Arthur, and that there
is not a true Englishman in England who is not a
Welshman. Pray take care of this letter, and do not lose
it out of your pocket, at least till you have left Wales.
I have seen one little dot of this great ball lately that
I had never seen before   Soon after your setting out
for Wales, I went to pass a couple of days with ——
at his living of —— ; his brother came over from
Cambridge to meet me.   It is a very comfortable
parsonage house, but too near a lord's house to please
me.   Rousseau says all grandeur is melancholy.   It
cannot be said that there is much grandeur in Lord

———'s house, unless the reverse of Rousseau's notion were also true, that whatever is melancholy is grand. The place is dismal in itself, and more so by comparison with what it was. The old lord was always at home, and very hospitable. Cicero says . ' Ampla domus dedecori domino sæpè fit, si est in eâ solitudo ; et maximè si aliquando alio domino solita est frequentari ; odiosum est enim cum à prætereuntibus dicitur, " O domus antiqua, heu quàm dispari dominare domino ! " ' an old line that always pleased me and stuck in my memory, and which I have often tacitly applied.

I thank you for Lowth. I have read the bishop's preliminary dissertation with pleasure, and some of the translation and notes. The information in the dissertation was new and curious to me ; I have not yet met with anything very striking in the notes, they seem now and then to be tritish. I dip at times into Jortin, but volumes of emendations are dry businesses ; and some authors seem to be mended that are scarce worth mending. But every author is a good author to a critic, if he is but sufficiently incorrect. The eighth Æneid, curâ Twiningi, is ready for you when you get home ; that is if you have been a good boy, and come home well from the mountains. I reckon you will be back in about a fortnight, the 9th of August. I go to Mr. Natt's for the week I long to know how you are I must take my leave now. Adieu. I hope my sister has been comforted

in her travels by good accounts of Mrs. Aldred , that
you are all three well, happy, and much amused. I
don't forget that I owe you answers to many things
in a long letter of yours ; and you shall have them
when you return.   Both our loves attend you.   I am
('excepto quod non simul essem, cætera lætus '), yours
affectionately,

T. T.

THE FAMILY NAME. — SENDING BOYS TO SCHOOL —
    EXAMPLE AND EMULATION. — NECESSITY OF
    SOCIETY, &c.

To his Brother.

Fordham, September 3, 1779

I thank you ; and for your Welsh letter, which
arrived safe, and was very acceptable to me.   I am
glad to think how pleasurable a journey you have
had, and how pleasurable a return.   My mouth is
wide open for your journal.   But, my dear sir, what
shall we do with this poor hackneyed name of ours ? [1]
For heaven's sake let us change it to Smith, or John-

---

[1] In Wales the name is pronounced 'Twinning.'   It is rather singular that upon a tour in South Wales, on reaching Llandrindod Wells,
as I drove up to the inn I saw a chariot standing at the door with my
crest upon it.   On inquiring to whom it belonged, I was told 'to the
Rev. Mr. Twinning,' who was a Pembrokeshire gentleman.—R. T.,
1818.

Our acquaintance with the Pembrokeshire 'Twinnings' then commenced was kept up to two succeeding generations.

Our name is spelt with two 'n's' in the indenture of Thomas
Twinning s (the founder of our business in the Strand) apprenticeship in
1694, but his signature has one 'n' only.—R. T., 1881.

son, or Webb, or something that is not quite so common and plebeian. Let us at least vamp it up, and give it a little gloss of novelty, by spelling it Tuineing, or Toeyenin, or Twoeyening, or Tooynynge, or something that shall sidle us away a little from those vulgar tribes of Western Twinings and Twynings. As I live, I thought no human creatures were distinguished by a more choice, gentlemanlike, rare, and curious appellation, than our family. But now! it puts me in mind of 'St. Amorous La Foole' in Ben Jonson : 'They all come out of our house, the La Fooles o' the north, the La Fooles of the west, the La Fooles of the east and south—we are as ancient a family as any in Europe, and we do bear our coat,' &c.

Little did I think when I permitted myself to abuse Welshmen, that I was a Welshman myself. We certainly are originally from thence. Well ; I am glad to find, however, that we have any origin ; that we are somebody, and came from somewhere. I think myself now a gentleman born, as Slender says, 'who may write himself 'Armigero in any bond, warrant,' &c. The two stars are certainly 'an old coat' The worst of it is, I cannot construe the Latin motto, but I suppose it means something handsome. But pray —don't these folks pronounce the name Twinning ? It is so pronounced in Wilts, where my estate is (some of our family have estates). I doubt the two babes and the 'gemelli' squint this way, as the serpents the other ; one pun for the visible, one for the audible word !

I see now what it is in my blood that makes me so immoderately fond of toasted cheese and onions, which are akin to leeks. What most mortifies me is, that anybody of the same name with me should have any resemblance to P——. 'Serpentes avibus geminantur, tigribus agni !' (Hor A. P.) Of all the tribe, I am most curious to see a Captain Twining, that there should be anything military in the family, anything that so much as ought only to have courage, is inconceivable. I hope for the honour of the name that the Pembrokeshire Militia will not be called to action. But, 'cedant arma togæ.' It seems a more feasible thing for a Twining to get learning than valour , and so let us talk of little Richard and his nouns and verbs Indeed, I shall not accuse you of fickleness ; I never understood that you meant to keep him long under your own tuition. I certainly never meant to advise you to it, though I may have expressed a wish that the education of children by their parents was a more feasible thing than it commonly is. Your reasons for not attempting it are all of them very strong and sufficient ; and, so far from wondering at your determination, I should very soon have begun to wonder on the other side of the question ; not that I think you a bit too late, I never saw any necessity for sending boys to school in such a hurry as is often done. But as you are kind enough to care about my opinion and approbation, I must say I think you will do right to find a school for Richard ere long. My reasons are exactly your own ; I need not repeat or add to them. The circumstance of play and play-fellows is not a trifling one. I believe society is as necessary to the improvement of a boy as of a man ; and it is not society, if it is not that of his equals. Harm, indeed, is got in all society, whether of men or boys ; but what animals should we be without it ? Compare a boy who has lived with a number of other boys, and one who has been kept at home, and had no such free intercourse with his equals as can be called associating with them. I believe you will find (*cæteris paribus*) the former boy to have more manli-ness, more spirit, more of that common sense and ex-perience that is so necessary to carry a man through life. I almost despair of being intelligible to you in this hasty scrawl. We know that all human improve-ment—everything that distinguishes civilised from savage men—has been owing to society, and men living with men. I believe there is certainly a differ-ence similar at least to this between boys in the two situations I speak of; a similar improvement to be got from their associating, I must be understood to mean, under proper regulation and inspection. I be-lieve Quinctilian (one of the most sensible men that ever wrote, and himself a schoolmaster) had the same idea that I have when he says :[1] ' Sensum ipsum qui

[1] Lib. i. Cap. 2, De Scholis.

communis dicitur ubi discet [*i.e* puer] cum se à con-
gressu, qui non hominibus solùm, sed mutis quoque
animalibus naturalis est segregârit ?' He adds admirably (for I find I must go on): 'Adde, quod domi
ea sola discere potest quæ ipsi præcipientur; in
scholâ etiam quæ aliis. Audiet multa quotidie pro-
bari, multa corrigi᠂ proderit alicujus objurgata de-
sidia, proderit laudata industria : excitabitur laude
æmulatio : turpe ducet cedere pari, pulchrum super-
asse majores.' This last point of example and emu-
lation is another great advantage of schools. That
they have also disadvantages nobody is more sensible
than I am. But, after all, to shut up every avenue to
corruption is impossible, at home or abroad. The
very idea of being able, by any care or management
whatever, to annihilate all risk of a boy's turning out
badly, is the wildest romance. Schools there must
be When you talk of Mr. Parr, I confess you meet
my wishes. I have often thought of it, but have been
restrained from saying anything, from the dread of
advising wrong in a matter of so much consequence,
and in which, as in inoculation, the inclinations of
parents ought to lead. Of Mr. Parr's abilities, learning, taste, manner of teaching, and finding out the
dispositions, talents, and characters of boys, I have the
highest idea. I have never met with such a man yet
in the shape of a schoolmaster. How he is in point
of discipline and severity I cannot pretend to say ; I
have been told that he flogs too much , but I doubt

F

those from whom I heard it think any use of punishment too much. In conversing with him, I have heard him disapprove of beating children. I have heard him say that words were his worst rod ; that what all his boys most dreaded was his talking to them, and shaming them before the whole school. This also is a delicate instrument of punishment ; and, injudiciously used, or carried too far, may do more harm than good. But I can hardly imagine that a man of his penetration and quickness in discerning the different tempers and characters of boys, should use this without proper discretion and distinction. Upon the whole, all I know is, that had I a son, and determined to send him to any school, I should certainly send him to Mr. Parr's. If one really means that a boy should learn to any purpose what one sends him to learn, surely it is of great importance that the master should be a man of sense and taste, able to convey those into the boys he teaches (if not deficient in capacity), and give them a relish of what they read. This, I am persuaded, is the case of Mr. Parr. Another reason that inclines me to wish Richard under his care is, the great regard and esteem which I am sure Mr. Parr has for me ; for, among other of his good qualities, he is a man of sincere and strong attachments. Richard seems to have a very good capacity, and is certainly amiable in his temper. If you resolve upon this step, I will write about it (if you choose it) to Mr. Parr ; and if you, who know Richard's temper and disposition much better than I can do, have any particular hints to give, I will convey them. To this last point Quinctilian also speaks well : 'In primis ea habenda est cura, ut is [the master] omnino fiat nobis familiariter amicus : nec officium in docendo spectet, sed effectum.' The circumstance of Norwich, likewise, is I suppose agreeable to my sister and you , I now wish more than ever that Mr. Parr had continued here.[1] Dr Forster has lately been to see Mr. Parr ; he is happier than ever he saw him ; has a large airy house, a noble schoolroom, and his school flourishes much. I must now cease. You shall hear again very soon.

CROAKING IN UNISON —NATIONAL ALARMS. —THE ENGLISH FLEET.—FEARS OF INVASION

To Dr. Burney.

Fordham, September 29, 1779

Bravissimo ! You really croak in a masterly manner considering the little time you have practised. I tried to get into unison with you—for who does not croak now ?—but could not get within an octave of your dismal hypo—hypo—hypo—hypo-dorian burden, the vibrations of which are as slow and desponding as the swings of a funeral bell, without

[1] The question here discussed was solved by my father's being sent to the High School at Norwich, under Dr. Parr, from whom my ather received an admirable education. He afterwards kept up a cordial intercourse with his old tutor both at Norwich and afterwards at Hatton, as long as he lived.—R T , 1881.

the accompaniment of a single harmonic to cheer
and brighten the note! It certainly belongs to the
hypo-chondriac mood. I am almost ashamed to joke
upon so serious a subject ; but though I lament the
situation which the unpardonable ignorance, or
neglect, or inability, or something worse than all
that of our managers have brought us into, and have
been visibly preparing for us—*de longue main* - yet
my prospect of things does not seem to be quite so
black as yours. My spirits are kept up by indignation , by a degree of restless, patriotic anxiety that I
never before experienced. I am too angry and too
eager to be low spirited. It comforts me and gives
me hopes to think that, though overpowered by
numbers, we still seem to keep up our superiority
in point of courage and resolution—our fighting
character. I firmly believe that great two-handed
bully, the combined fleet, was and is afraid to meet
our inferior force—afraid to provoke us by attempting
anything upon our coasts. If I were to be in a room
with Admiral Barrington I should prostrate myself at
his feet. This last American smash of Sir Geo.
Collier's is fine. I hope—I hope—we are rousing,
and beginning to be in earnest. I look up to Admiral
Ross with greater confidence, perhaps, than cool reflection will warrant , in short, my wishes are so
strong that they draw my hopes after them. As for
pleasures, comforts, and conveniences, I thank God
I miss none yet that I am used to or desire ; nor do

I see much alteration round me, except what arises from the imprudence of those who suffer. I am up and down, sometimes higher, sometimes lower, as things strike me. I am 'Jean qui rit, et Jean qui pleure.' When, in one column of a newspaper, I read of some ill-success or threatening manœuvre of the enemy, 'je pleure;' but when I see, in the next, assemblies, concerts, and races advertised, servants wanted who can dress hair, &c., 'je ris.' 'We cannot,' quoth I to myself, 'be in the dangerous situation some people talk of; for who then would care whether his hair had pomatum and powder in it or not? Who would dance if the French and Spaniards were invading us?' &c. I am comforted even when I see a new blacking for shoes advertised Aristotle? 'Tis really, as you say, ridiculous at such a time to think such futilities of any importance. Yet, as I must employ myself in some literary way, I do get on; but at a snail's pace. 'Tis digging work, and I am afraid of tiring myself. The worst of it is, the book is in such a pickle that a man can never know, in any given page of it, whether he is translating Aristotle or a rat! . . . For one thing I weep, *à chaudes larmes*, Houghton[1]—ah!

Yours,   T. T.

[1] The sale of that famous gallery of pictures to the Empress Catherine of Russia, and its loss to this country.

THE SCHOOL QUESTION SETTLED —A NEW TIBULLUS.
—SOME FRIENDLY CRITICISMS.

To his Brother.

Fordham, October 17, 1779.

I must write you a word by my mother , but it must be pithy and laconic.   It is late , I am lazy ; and to-morrow morning we go to Colchester, to pass as much of the day as we can with my mother.

I hope you were happy in the conversation of Dr. ——.   It must comfort and cheer you through all the fatigues of the day to think of the refreshment that was prepared for your evening.   Did not you say to yourself, ' O ! te, Bolane, cerebri felicem !' The man has a Welsh name, however ; that was something.   And if he should fall in love with you, that may be something more   I have had a good, longish letter from Mr. Parr, and I can read it all except some half-dozen words, though I have not had it above a fortnight ! [1]   He says 'he shall most readily take my nephew under his friendly and affectionate care.'   Then follows a bit of Greek about equality, impartiality, &c., which I can't half decipher. Then he says, ' Depend upon it that he will receive from me, in the highest ' (I think it is—but ?) ' degree, that treatment which is due to the son of your brother and the nephew of a man who is in himself, and to

[1] Mr. (Dr) Parr's handwriting was decipherable only with the utmost difficulty.

me, what you are.' Do you see, sir?—we are somewhat accounted of! I am very glad to find, by my
mother, that dear Richard [1] is, at present, well pleased
with his new situation. I did not at all like the
thoughts of my sister and her little fellow-traveller
being so near me without my seeing them ; but it
could not well be helped.

I thank you much for the Tibullus—by far the
most elegant German book I ever saw. The vignettes
please me much, and the author, you know, is a
favourite with me. I said, as I put him upon my
shelf, 'Thank heaven, you are neither a quarter of
house lamb, nor a turkey!'

Your journal has amused me and Mrs. T. prodigiously. We have travelled every evening with
you—Camden upon the table. I thank you for
improving me ; for I have certainly got some knowledge, and some ideas, which I had not before. I
seem to myself to have as clear a conception of North
Wales as can be got without actual sight, which will
never be my lot.[2] It is my lot to live upon a trencher,
and once or twice in my life to mount, with great
difficulty, upon a mole-hill, and fancy myself in the
clouds. Nobody can imagine how I abominate a
level country. I like vastly your idea of Radnorshire,
and how it came to be Radnorshire, and many more

[1] My father's first going to school at Dr. Parr's, Norwich.—R. T.,
1881.
[2] It was his lot, in the year 1797 ; and for his thorough enjoyment
of it, see his Journal further on.

of your ideas, observations, descriptions, &c. This is
certainly your tip-top journal—*rebus* and *verbis* But
two things misliked me in the whole journal. You
somewhere use a form of reference that I abominate,
i.e., the latter, the former. It may have its con-
venience sometimes ; yet I find myself always forced
to look back, and see which is which ; and, moreover,
there is an appearance always of aiming at antithesis.
I don't mean that you had any such aim , you write
better than all that comes to , but the form is used
by your little dapper writers, who mean to write
prettily—ergo, should never be used by you. 'As
long as you have the use of your tongue and your
pen,' said Dr. Johnson to Dr. Burney, 'never, sir, be
reduced to that shift !' The second thing is your
character of Warburton. 'Learned' does not charac-
terise him ; it confounds him with the Bentleys and
the Burmans. Learning implies skill in ancient
languages. Many exceeded the Bishop in that. His
character was uncommon ingenuity, bright parts,
and great general knowledge, ancient and modern.
Learned, you see, would not convey these ideas.
Bishop Pearce was a far more learned man than
Warburton, with no genius at all But I must stop.
Adieu ! I hope to talk these matters with you.
Cannot Fordham be your inn as you go? Let me
hear on Saturday or Thursday ; both days (this
week) I shall be in town.—Yours affectionately,

T. T.

'ORIENTAL JONES.'—UNEASINESS OF THE TIMES.—
A FIDDLING PARTY.

To Dr. Burney.

Fordham, November 3, 1779.

I don't know Oriental[1] Jones ; but by what I have
heard of him I conceive him to be far from a mere
linguist—a man of sense, taste, and humour.   This
last I conclude from a character I have in MS. of his
writing in Greek in imitation of Theophrastus, in
which he has grouped together all the particularities
of a friend of mine (Parr, who was usher at Harrow
School), with a good deal of fun, and in very good
and very Theophrastic Greek.   Of Tamerlane's mo-
ralities I have no very great notion.   Moral maxims
are apt to be as tiresome to read as they are important to practice.

    .   .   .   .   .   .

Some anxiety about our situation !   I am as
anxious as you can be, though perhaps not quite
so desponding, though I believe we are not above
a flat third asunder.   I was never disposed to join in
the popular grumble against the Ministry ; but now
the force of evidence has turned me fairly round
This will be an ignominious reign in the history of
the country.

Do I grumble well ? . . . The author is ——,
a very sensible, agreeable man ; but tinctured with

---

[1] The learned and accomplished Orientalist, Sir William Jones.

some prejudices very unphilosophical for a philosopher. He is very orthodox in religion, and very
heterodox in philosophy. But he is a searching,
experimentising, active-minded man, and deserves to
be—what he never will be—free from prejudices of
all sorts.

Colchester, January 6, 1780.

Your letter found me out—that is, it did not find
me out—that is, it found me out of Colchester—that
is, it did not find me at all, nor I it, till I came back
on Saturday last, *sçavoir*, from my usual week of
musical society at Mr. Bramston's, where we fiddled
de randonnée.

VISITS TO CONCERTS. —MISS HARROP'S SINGING.—
PACCHIEROTTI, THE TENOR.

To Dr. Hey.

Colchester, February 24, 1780

As I think you told me you were to preach at
Whitehall on the 20th, I take it for granted this will
find you in the great city, which I have just left, and
je m'en trouve bien. I seem to have abundance of
things to say to you, of one sort or other. I hoped
you would have arrived in town the beginning of
last week, and that we might have had one opera
together, and perhaps have met at Bach's concert
on the Wednesday. Elmsall was in town a week ;
we were much together, and wished for you *ardem-*

ment, as a Frenchman would call it. We were together at two operas—Contadina in Corte, &c., and Q. Fabio ; at Bach's concert ; and we dined with Bates one day, and heard Miss Harrop sing from tea-time till ten o'clock ; snug and comfortable ; no audience but the two Bates's, Mrs. Bates, and ourselves. One of the greatest musical treats I ever had. I had, as Sir Hugh Evans says, 'great dispositions to cry ;' nay, the tears actually came out, and Elmsall said he should have cried if he had not seen how foolish I looked. She sung Pergolesi, Leo, Hasse—things I know, and that nobody sings. It gave me some faint idea of meeting one's departed friends in heaven. I was thrice at Bach's concert. Imagine how I was pleased to hear Miss Harrop begin 'Nel chiuso centro,' &c., my old favourite cantata of Pergolesi, which I never expected to hear so sung and so accompanied ! She sang only the first verse and air. Afterwards, at Bates's, she went through the whole. She has every sort of expression. She sung the last angry, despairing air with vast spirit and sympathy. I can find nothing like a fault, except a little timidity, caution, taking breath, and other symptoms of *apprêt* and teaching in her cadences. Well, but Pacchierotti ! *C'en est fait.* I confess I have never been so charmed and interested by any singer of this class. Your disliking [1]

[1] Note by Dr. Hey.—'The singing of Mrs. Bates and Pacchierotti.' The latter I had heard the year before, and was not sufficiently pleased

him so much had great weight with me. It did not
quite overset all the expectations that Dr. Burney's
account had raised in me ; but it made me despair
of being very highly pleased, though I expected to
like Pacchierotti better than you did   I went to the
opera in a state as near perfect neutrality as I
could put myself in.   I began to hear as Descartes
would have one begin to reason.   In his (not Descartes') first line of recitative his voice and manner
got immediate hold of me.   I shuffled forward upon
my seat, and said to myself, ' This is superior singing.'
Quid multis ?   I heard him six times, one of which
was at Dr. Burney's, in a snug way.   I liked him
better and better, and do think that for taste, spon-
taneous variation, delicacy, and expression, he is far
beyond any singer I have heard.   His voice, though
not strong, and liable to variation, is to my ear sweet
with a very peculiar sort of sweetness.   In gracing,
he does the most beautiful, most unassignable, most
unwritten and unwriteable things I ever heard ; there
seems no end of his fancy ; and all—at least, most of
it—is evidently *sur-le-champ.*   He also seems to me
to feel more than any singer I remember, and though

with him. His voice seemed husky, and he sometimes sung out of
tune (both are owned in the letter), still I suppose he was very
masterly.   I always said with great sincerity that the defect was in me,
and not in him.   I think so still   I never defended my feelings, I
only simply expressed them.   I was not up to judging how far his
graces were from sentiment at the time; but no graces can make me
amends for the loss of melody, simple, good in itself, and feelingly expressed.—J. H.

his fancy and his flexibility of voice lead him sometimes into an intemperance of ornament, yet I never
heard any singer who could give such expression as
he often does to a few simple notes. His recitative
is delightful. For instance (I suppose you will hear
Q Fabio), observe one line of recitative, 'Apri
quei vaghi lumi,' in the sixth scene of the third act,
where he finds Emilia in a swoon. There is a very
fine song in the second act, 'Ma pria ch'io rieda al
campo.' He is equally excellent, I think, in the
proud and tender expression of it ; but, in particular,
will you say you ever heard anything more delicious
than his manner of singing this passage, in itself very
common ?—

I know that things of this kind must be lost upon
people who are not advanced to a certain degree in
music. I do not expect simple hearers to be pleased.
But you ! Surely Pacchierotti must sing much better
(better, everybody says) this winter than the last, or
he must have got at you, now and then, at least. If
you think me prejudiced, you will not think Elmsall
prejudiced, and he was delighted : 'What can Hey
mean,' quoth he, 'by not liking this ? ' I confess I
was much pleased to find we heard in perfect sympathy. I did not expect him to be so much pleased
as I was. I don't deny that Pacchierotti has faults.

He sometimes sings a note too flat ; though but very
seldom, whenever I have heard him. He sometimes
does too much ; is exuberant and wanton. But to
have too much fancy and invention is so rare a fault !
His cadences are often not quite what one would
expect from the rest of his singing ; I liked him less
there than anywhere. When I heard him in a room
I was surprised to find his voice husky. In his first
song he was so hoarse that it was pain to hear him.
He had no cold ; but he is liable to a sudden pain in
his stomach, which affects his voice, and in a song or
two goes off. I should suppose it some weakness of
this sort that makes him liable to sing high notes too
flat. At best, his voice in a room has a very different
effect from what it has upon the stage ; it wants distance to deliver it bright and clear to the ear. Mr.
Burney says this is more or less the case with all
castrato voices ; they will not do close to your ear
like a woman's voice. I was much pleased with
Pacchierotti as a man and a conversible creature.
He seems to have a great deal of sense, sensibility,
taste, and modesty ; loves English, and studies it, as
he expresses it, 'hardly.' Mason takes much notice
of him. He has read Pope, &c, and is now reading
Hume's history, &c., &c. ; for those little things will
serve to talk of some day at Easton, Fordham, Passenham, &c. I must pull in, or my letter will never
end. The comic opera, I think, is in a sad plight as
to singers.—Yours,   T. T.

PACCHIEROTTI—ADMIRAL RODNEY AND THE SPANISH FLEET.

To Dr. Burney.

Colchester, March 22, 1780.

Your specimens of Provençal melody are delightful, curious, gratifying; fruit for every musical palate, gathered fresh with your own hand out of your own garden. The whole, indeed, pleases me much, and I think will please all readers of any reasonable curiosity or taste.

.   .   .   .   .   .

I rejoiced to hear Pacchierotti had so good a benefit, and so much applause. How much I am obliged to you for procuring me a meeting with him in so snug and comfortable a way. Nay, how much I am obliged to you all, good souls as you are, for all your *bel accueil*, mutton chops, conversation, punch, &c. I will be free to say that I don't know anywhere such a house full of ' &c.' It truly mortifies me that I cannot be more with you than I am while I stay in town ; but 'tis all scramble and distraction. Well, but has not Admiral Rodney given a good account of the Spanish fleet! Have not we done great things since the beginning of the winter ? Do not our prospects brighten ? Considering the powerful league against us, and our unallied condition, I don't think we ever made a more respectable figure. I want nothing but one good smash at the French fleet.—Yours sincerely,   T. T.

THE LORD GEORGE GORDON RIOTS.

From Dr. Burney to the Rev. T. Twining.

Sunday, May 11, 1780.

Ah, my ever dear and worthy friend, into what a
situation are we brought by the pusillanimity of one
party and the malignity of another !   The newspapers
must have told you of the outrages committed by Lord
G. Gordon's mob on public buildings and persons of
high rank, as well as of the general confusion that
has reigned here ever since Friday sennight, when he
was suffered to muster and head the fanatics in St.
George's Fields ; but you can have no conception of
the particular consternation, distress, and danger into
which the inhabitants of Newton House[1] have been
involved by the fury of the miscreants who, on
Monday night, assaulted the house of Sir George
Saville, in Leicester Fields, and on Tuesday that of
Justice Hyde, in our very street ; making bonfires of
their furniture, and in this last not leaving a floor, a
shutter, door, window-frame, or anything which could
feed six or seven fires in the street at first, and afterwards one great fire at the top of it, in Leicester
Fields, from six in the evening till two o'clock the
next morning ; at the same time obliging all the
inhabitants to illuminate for this victory over all law
and government ; while Newgate was broken open,

[1] Dr. Burney's residence.

two or three hundred prisoners set at liberty, and the building set on fire. Wednesday night will be remembered by all the present inhabitants of London and Westminster to their latest hour for the horrors and calamities with which it abounded. The furniture, books, and MSS. of Lord Mansfield had been destroyed in the morning, together with his house in town, when himself and lady narrowly escaped with their lives. Caen Wood had likewise been devoted and beset, but was preserved by a regiment of militia. However, at night there were no less than five or six dreadful fires raging at the same instant. The King's Bench, Marshalsea and Fleet Prisons, the dwelling-house, shop, and distillery of a Roman Catholic in Holborn, the house of another in Great Queen Street, and of a third in the Poultry—all these and more furnished a sight from my observatory, particularly that of the distillery, which surpassed the appearance of Mount Vesuvius in all its fury. There was not, I believe, during this day and night a thinking or sober inhabitant in any part of the town who was a house-keeper, or in possession of anything valuable, that thought himself safe. Every one moved his papers and most valuable effects to the dwelling of some friend, whose situation was equally dangerous; for what street or quarter of the town could be found without a justice of peace, a judge, a minister of state, an ambassador, a bishop, or a Roman Catholic? The houses and furniture of all these were devoted to the

G

flames ; and, unluckily for me in particular, one of
the tenants of two tenements adjoining to my house,
and part of the same estate, is a Roman Catholic,
and among the proscribed, so that whatever is the
fate of his habitation will be that of mine ! The
first things I removed to the house of a friend were
the valuable books and MSS. which had been lent to
me ; the next some writings to another ; and thirdly,
a coachfull of the MSS. I had collected for my
' History' in France, Italy, Germany, and elsewhere
during my travels, and the greatest part of my life, I
sent to Mr. Burney, supposing him in a quiet part of
the town, and intending to send more ; but the second
load was brought back, as likely to be more safe in
my own house, there being a riot in his street, and
a banditti levying money at pleasure of the inhabitants !

Thursday things remained pretty quiet, after the
military ventured to fire at these free-born English-
men on their attempting the Bank. The blue
cockades, however, those signals of sedition, rapine,
and plunder, abounded in the streets, to my great
annoyance and astonishment, till evening, when near
a hundred of the perpetrators of all these mischiefs
being found drunk about Fleet Ditch, were secured ;
and a proclamation published that the soldiers were
ordered to fire on all rioters without waiting for a
civil magistrate to read the Riot Act. With a rumour
that martial law would be enforced, not a vestige of

the 2,500*l.* worth of blue ribbon purchased by Lord George Gordon and his friends was to be seen in the streets Friday and yesterday all was quiet in London and Westminster, except the seizing delinquents, and entering the house of one More, a rascally printer, who dispersed handbills to encourage the friends of Lord Gordon and Protestantism to liberate him from the Tower. In the Borough, however, there were disturbances both these days ; and even yesterday three or four fires were made in one of the streets with the furniture and effects of an unfortunate Roman Catholic. However, at night all seemed perfectly quiet, and I was one of the few who ventured to go to the Opera, where all the performers, being guilty of a religion and country different from the mad bull John, sung and danced with the utmost fear and trembling ; yet Pacchierotti is as superior in courage to the rest as in talents. He says that he should be much more frightened in Italy or anywhere else than England during such disturbances, as the English are not sanguinary upon these occasions. No soldiers could be spared for the usual opera guard, and all was melancholy and forlorn. I began, however, to tranquillise, and imagine all was over , but alas, like a new cap, the mischief is gone into the country ! for an express arrived last night from Bath in eight hours, with the news of the colliers having entered that city, beaten the Queen's Rangers who were quartered there, and imitating all the outrages against the poor defenceless Catholics which have been practised in London ! . . . Where will all this end ? and what is it for ?   The Protestants feel no more inconvenience from the tolerating Bill in favour of Papists, than from the Talmud or Alcoran ; and the cry of ' No Popery' can only be construed into ' No Loyalty' and 'No King !'   The Oliverian and Republican spirit is gone forth, and religion is a mere pretence for subverting the Government and destroying the Constitution.   This should be more generally known and counteracted than it is by the friends of Church and State.

Your kindest of all letters arrived before all this violence and fury began to rage openly, and comforted, pleased, and amused me beyond measure.

C B.

REFLECTIONS ON THE GORDON RIOTS.—OBJECTIONS TO MILITARY INTERFERENCE.

The Rev. T. Twining to Dr. Burney.

Fordham, June 16, 1780.

Suave mari magno turbantibus æquora ventis
E terra magnum alterius spectare laborem, etc.

The lines are pleasant, though somewhat the worse for wear.   But this same suavity is but a shabby kind of suavity at best ; and very shabby indeed when our friends are in the storm ; and so I can't say I have tasted a bit more of this sugar than just what self has crammed into my mouth whether I would or no. But look ye ; you have been, I dare say, and are, too much hurried to write long letters ; but I must and will know directly how you all do, how you have weathered this horrid storm, &c.[1] I hope not a hair of your heads, nor a pane of your windows has suffered harm ; frightened, I doubt not, you have all been sufficiently. Good God ! what a scene ! for my part, I believe I shall never get my hair out of the perpendicular again as long as I live ! At this time of day ; in a philosophic, enlightened age, as it is called ! What punishment is too much for an endeavour to inflame a people with religious animosities ? especially at such a time, when that kind of spirit has long been quietly laid , and mankind in general, if left to themselves, have little or no propensity to that most horrible of all vices called zeal. I congratulate you upon the appearance of peace and protection at last. I am in hopes that good consequences may follow this convulsion, that it may a little help to open people's eyes, and to bring into disgrace the associating spirit, by showing so evidently its only tendency. One thing, I own, gave me some degree of pleasure ; that as mischief was done, some of it fell on the patriotic side. I am no party man ; but there is a justice in their feeling a little of the effects of that spirit of sedition which they have been

---

[1] The Lord George Gordon Riots, 1780. See also Dr. Burney's letter.

so ready to encourage; for even to talk of it, or to hint at it, is I think to encourage it. Well, the detestable leader of this business is at present secured. Can anything be so absurd as to talk or think of quelling such a riot as this by the civil power? If it had not been for the army, what would have become of us? It is still inconceivable to me how so much mischief has been done, considering that houses are not stripped and pulled down in a minute, and that a small number of armed men, with proper resolution, could I suppose disperse very soon the largest unarmed mob. They cannot stand against bullets I am puzzled. Surely Lord Mansfield's house might have been saved? Now, I will lay you a wager—I beg pardon; I pledge myself—that when the House meets you will have fine orations against calling in the military, martial law, &c.

OUTCRY AGAINST 'MILITARY GOVERNMENT.'— THE POPULAR LOVE OF LIBERTY. — PROTESTANT 'TOLERATION.'—FOREIGN AFFAIRS.

To Dr. Burney.

Fordham, July 14, 1780.

Your kind and communicative letter was most acceptable to me. I hope my letter of enquiry that met it upon the road, and in some sort, and as a body may say, answered it before it was received, has served as some excuse with you for my silence, which would not otherwise have been so long. Alas! I had not any idea of the peculiar danger my friends at Newton House were in ; and when I knew it, I was quite shocked to think that I should have suffered the least giggle, grin, or smirk to be seen upon the countenance of my letter. I was glad, however, that I knew your danger only when it was over. Thank God all was soon quieted by the military ; and I hope the examples that have been made, and will be made, will keep all quiet Though, for my own part, I care not how long we are under this dreadful military government, about which such a ridiculous clamour is made It is astonishing to me how any man can have the audacity to express a wish at such a time for the removal of protection. I can scarce command my candour to believe that those who talk in that manner would not be rather pleased to see the renewal of the disturbances The civil power ! what is the civil power ? a power that will be civil to a mob, as the Lord Mayor was ? Is a mob of thousands to be dispersed by the gold-headed cane of a justice of the peace, or a parcel of sticks painted at one end ? If they can be repelled only by an armed force, those in whose hands arms are put must be trusted, let them be who they will ; and, for my part, I should think myself much safer in the protection of the army than of my fellow-citizens, considering the unaccountable spirit of sedition and political malignity that prevails amongst them. I have often said it, and I do think it, that we are the most discontented, ill-humoured, black-blooded, unthankful people upon earth, and deserve to be ruled with a rod of iron. In nine out of ten of us at least the love of liberty, of which we boast so much, is nothing but the hatred of liberty in others, and the desire of tyranny for ourselves. It is impatience of all restraint. It is ill-humour, malignity, &c. Fontenelle says admirably : ' Le sentiment de la liberté est plus vif, plus il y entre de malignité.' Your true Englishman is never so happy as under a bad government. A perfect administration, could the experiment be tried, would dislocate the jaws of above half his Majesty's good subjects with ennui. Though, why so? they would make grievances though an angel were minister, and an archangel king. To be sure, if we were under the most despotic and cruel government upon earth, if a man could not marry his daughter without asking Lord North's leave, could not take a journey without being escorted by a King's messenger, or was obliged to take out a licence on stamped paper for every tune he plays upon his fiddle or pianoforte, &c.—we could not make a greater outcry than we do, or be in a more incessant grumble. As to toleration, we are children yet ; the very word proves it ; religious liberty can never be upon its right footing while that word exists. Tolerate !—it is a word of insult. Suppose a man should say to you when you were commending Pacchierotti, ' Sir, your opinion is very different from mine, but, however, I shall put up with it.' The world, if it last some thousand years longer, will begin perhaps to find out the folly and mischief and inutility of paying any regard to each other's opinions and principles, *as* such ; that they have nothing to do but with action and conduct. Here are a parcel of fanatical, persecuting Papal Protestants who would treat all the Papists in the kingdom as bad subjects and dangerous men, because they would be so, if their conduct was perfectly consistent with the spirit of their religion, or rather what was once the spirit of it. It is curious to reflect—or would be, if it were not shocking—that if the populace had not been opposed, in all probability the massacre of Paris would have been acted over again, by Protestants, in the massacre of London ! No ; Christianity, my dear friend, does not give any sort of encouragement to the cutting one another's throats at all ; but I know this, that the Papist who cuts throats upon religious principle, bad and mistaken as it is, has less to answer for than the Protestant who does it in direct repugnance to all principle, religious and moral. Oh, how I preach ! I beg your pardon ; but these matters fill me with indignation when I think of them. I am pretty confident that you and I are as well agreed upon these, as we are upon other points. We have been all peace in this part of the world. The association for redress of grievances, with your friend —— in the chair, has been silent and inactive of late I

hope this associating spirit will be quenched by the
terrible effect of the Protestant Association. It must
open the eyes of many well-meaning people who had
before joined in them.

.   .   .   .   .

Come, come, we have taken Charlestown, the rebels
are hard pushed. Rodney is a noble fellow, and can
do everything but command the winds. Heaven send
the Spanish fleet into his jaws! Without much straining of one's eyes, I hope we may think we see Peace,
with her plump cheeks, and her cornucopia full of
carrots and cabbages and good garden stuff, coming
at a distance So you may write on ; the world will
be ready for you ere you have finished, and we shall
sit under our vines and fig-trees with our swords beat
into ploughshares, and our spears into pruning-hooks,
and we shall read of music and poetry, and the arts
of peace, good humour, and amusement , and sing
and fiddle and divert ourselves, and tear all books
on solemn, ill-humoured, quarrelsome topics into
slips to put round our candles, and light our pipes ;
and this happy state will last a great while—ay, for
two or three years for aught I know, and then we
shall all begin to grow sour again, and fall together
by the ears like a pack of bull-dogs. Have your
book, ready, therefore, to throw in, like the bark,
between the fits I am glad your sheet was proof
against Dr Johnson's criticism. I believe his eulo-
gium to be strictly true, and I hope you felt yourself

filliped on by it. Oh, and so your friend has been
pushing towards the legislative line, and has not
succeeded, I hear. It seems he is a patriot; if so,
I cannot be sorry, for we have patriots enough. It
is a grievous thing for this poor country that so many
people love it !

_____

THE PLEASURES OF A PARCEL OF BOOKS.—ENGLAND
AND 'THE DUTCH.'

To his Brother.

Colchester, January 8, 1781

I owe you an appendix to my last letter : I wish
all debts were as willingly paid. I was much diverted
last night at the opening of the two parcels that
arrived in Mills's goods. I hope you saw the con-
tents ; there never was a more complete contrast
Out first comes Julius Cæsar Scaliger; ' It should
be Julius Cæsar scavenger ! ' quoth I, to myself. But
when the splendid back and the more splendid belly
of the other book appeared, I started back. It was
a perfect emblem of the unequal distribution of things
in this world. Two things I have always hated—dirt
and finery. The mixture is ten times worse than
either separately ; but when finery includes cleanli-
ness it fairly deserves the preference to dirt—and so
I like my beau book better than my sloven. Nay,
there is a simplicity in the gilding of his back that
likes me much, and is new to me   If the leaves had
been green the book would have been within the

bounds of the 'simplex munditiis'! One can never be in time for Payne! My principal lots were gone. Yet I lost no time. To do the fair thing, Payne ought not to begin selling till his catalogue has had time to reach his most distant correspondent. He gives us country bookworms no chance. Pray, when you walk that way, see if No. 4417 or 4418 (if not too fine) are to be had; for I am not worth an Apollonius Rhodius. If these are gone, let me have 1915, Horapollinis, &c. If all are flown, I sulk, and will look no farther. I am very well pleased with my Ernestus, though I am sorry it has been in the possession of a slovenly blockhead, who, I dare be sworn, has left more in the book than the book has left in him. I was disappointed to find that the edition is Clark's reprinted, with the addition of some short notes, and not numerous, of Ernestus. Still, as it has all Clark's notes, and Ernestus's added, and very good indexes, &c, it is a better edition, and I by no means repent of my purchase. While I think of it—if in glancing your eye over catalogues it should hitch upon Rymer's translation of Aristotle's Poetics, with Rapin's notes from the French, 1674, 8vo, buy it for me. A translator likes to see what others have done before him. I knew of this English translation but lately. Also, pray ask Elmsley if he has got Condillac's 'Essai sur l'Origine des Connaissances Humaines,' two small vols., an excellent metaphysical work, and which I must purchase some time

or other. I am reading it, with much pleasure, upon
Dr. Forster's recommendation. I will send your
Virgilian MS., &c., by the coach on Wednesday,
and with them a little book of Erasmus's which you
may find useful among your auxiliaries. ' Est etiam
in parvo munere, dantis amor.' Dear me ! I have
duty to present to you from Mr. Bramston's butler,
whose name is Money (or sounds so), and who lived,
it seems, with our poor friend Humfrey.[1] I hope he
has a comfortable place there. Mr B. has at present
a very good opinion of him. We passed a most
pleasant week at Skreens. Everybody is pleased
with our spirited attack upon the Dutch, except
determined croakers and the lovers of despair. It
is certainly a bold stroke ; but in some cases bold-
ness is prudence. Even so short-sighted a political
eye as mine can see many good reasons for this
measure, even in point of policy and prudence We
have already done the Dutch very great damage, and
I do not see how they can be able, in any tolerable
time, to do as much.—Yours affectionately,

T. T.

[1] The Rev. Richard Humfrey, a most valued friend of the family.
He was preceptor to two of George III.'s younger sons, and was generally resident either at St. James's Palace or Kew. He died after a
short illness at Thorpe, near Norwich, circa 1780.

THE ACQUITTAL OF LORD GEORGE GORDON.

To Dr. Burney.

Colchester, February 12, 1781.

And so Lord George Gordon is acquitted, and all the world seems as much delighted as if he had been the most innocent and most oppressed of men! Now, for my part, I cannot get myself to be the least glad about the matter; and I do think you feel much as I do. What 'legal' treason is—high or low—I know not; nor whether this man has been guilty of it or not. One thing is tolerably clear to me—that the good of society, the safety of society, fairly requires that any man who does what he did should be hanged, call it treason or call it anything else. What is to become of us if any man may with impunity assemble 40,000 people, and tell them that the King had broken his coronation oath, *i.e.*, that they were absolved from their allegiance? But it is the sweetest, best humoured, and most compassionate age that we live in! There are now no crimes; they are all frailties, misfortunes. There were the 'unfortunate' Perreaus, the 'unfortunate' Dr. Dodd; here is an 'unfortunate' young nobleman. Forging a note and raising a sedition are unlucky accidents to which every man is liable, just as he may fall down and break his leg. If I was a satirist, and had a mind to say a very severe thing, supported by some truth, I would say that the present age has left itself but one virtue—humanity; and that it has turned into a vice by its abuse of it!—Yours, T. T.

SPECULATIONS ON A FOREIGN TOUR.—RAMBLES AT
HOME.—HALIFAX AND TODMORDEN.—A GERMAN
SUPERSTITION.

To his Brother.

Fordham, from August 9, 1781, to the 18th.

I have not heard that you have left old England,
for I have heard nothing ; but I take it for granted
you have, and that this letter will find you all safely
lodged at Spa, very busy and very happy. I hope
your neutral bottom protected you well, and that ye
have not been frighted by French, Spaniards, or
Dutch. Sick enough, poor creatures, I know ye all
have been. Let me hope, too, that the sea has left
you bowels enough to go on comfortably, and eyes
enough (though somewhat 'elisos' by straining) to
look about you ! All this, I *suppose*, for the present ;
but shall be impatient to have it confirmed. *En
attendant*, let me tell you that we arrived safe at
Fordham on Friday evening last, after a journey as
pleasant as a great deal too much dust and a little
too much heat would permit. I hope you will have
heard before this reaches you that I mended from
the time I wrote to you last ; was very comfortable
during my journey, and have continued so till now.
Knowing how much you would wish for a better
account of me, I wrote to my mother, on my arrival
at home, desiring that whoever first wrote to you
would mention it.

I write by bits and scraps, as the humour takes me. During my pause after the fatigues of the first page, arrived your welcome letter. Thanks. You can't think how odd 'Ostend' looked at the top of it; I firmly believe you wrote it in your closet at Twickenham. But no matter for that, I am determined to believe all you write, if only for my own amusement. How I envy you that state of perfect novelty which you are now in! The saying that there is nothing new under the sun is a comfortable doctrine to us poor creatures whose lot it is to be tethered down for life to one spot, by a rope of only a few scanty hundreds of miles in length. You are on the Continent? Very well, then you are upon a larger island than I am upon—that's all. You see men and women, I suppose, such as I see; the trees consist of leaves and branches, and the grass is green; the buildings, I imagine, are of stone, brick, or wood; cows are cows, and horses horses. 'There is nothing new under the sun.' A little variety of combination is all you can boast of; the materials are the same. Is it worth a wise man's while to expose himself to the dangers of the ocean only to see cloth differently made up, or hear a different arrangement of the same elements of speech? Give me a country where the trees grow bottom upwards, with their foliage in the ground and their roots sprawling in the air; or where men converse by blowing their noses in different tones and articulations, or express violent grief by a horse laugh, and cry when they are merry. This would be something new under the sun.

Well; but let me now tell you what I have seen. I can be contented with combinations new to me, and such I have seen—combinations, I mean, of trees, rocks, and water chiefly. Our first ramble from Emley was to a village called Todmorden, about twenty-eight miles off, upon the very confines of Lancashire, part of it in Lancashire. This was for the sake of seeing the country from Halifax to Todmorden (pronounced Tawmorden). Our route lay through Huddersfield, Ealand, Halifax, and Hepton Bridge. The whole ride from Huddersfield is a climax of rich and beautiful country. There is a new road made from Huddersfield to Ealand, along the side of the Calder, by which many terrible tugs over the hills are avoided; and you are well paid for the loss of some great staring prospects by the nearer, more distinct, and picturesque views of the lower road. This is—great part of it—cut through a thick wood hanging down to the river, which you see glittering through the boughs under you on your left, a woody and rocky steep rising on your right, the little falls in the river producing a perpetual rustle of water, and the effects of the whole varying at every bend of the road There is still a considerable descent to Ealand, and a magnificent view. The weather was cloudy and unsettled; just as the view opened it began to rain. The little I could look at, with the head of the chaise

H

in my way, was veiled in mist. I murmured sadly ; it answered, for the rain stopped. A little gleam of sunshine, through an opening cloud at the extremity of a long vale on the left, came stealing along, till by slow degrees the whole valley and the town were illuminated, part of the surrounding hills still remaining in shade and forming a sort of black frame to this bright and beautiful picture. I never felt anything so fine. I shall remember it, and thank God for it, as long as I live. I am sorry I did not think to say grace after it Are we to be grateful for nothing but beef and pudding ?—to thank God for life, and not for happiness ?

We drank tea at Ealand ; took a peep of the view, which I found as fine as ever ; then went on to Halifax, an excellent road of two miles and a half, close to the side of the river, along a winding vale into which other vales open, all hung with woods, rocks peeping through, &c. Slept at Halifax I think you have not been there. The town is nothing extraordinary, except for the many magnificent houses lately built, and now daily building, in and about it, by the manufacturers chiefly The appearance of trade, population, and advancement of every kind there is striking The town is in a bottom with monstrous hills about it, which you see rising over the houses as you walk the streets.

The Cloth Hall is a new and magnificent stone building a square of 100 yards each side, consisting of a great court with piazzas all round, and little rooms or shops belonging to different traders ; for I cannot describe buildings. But the inside is very magnificent ; and such a busy scene on the market day I never saw, a perpetual stream to and from it of men carrying bundles of cloth, &c., &c. The ground being uneven, there are three stories on the lower side and only two, I think, on the others, which is thought a blemish I can't say it hurt my eye much. There are pillars and galleries one above another. It presents a strange appearance without ; contented with ornamenting the inside, they have left the outside without the least bit of pillar, pilaster, window, ornament, or break of any kind, except the front and entrance of the building. Think how queer, one hundred yards of dead stone wall presented to your eye !

I should not have expected to meet with a bookseller [1] in Halifax who is one of the best and most elegant binders in England, and has a valuable collection of books and prints. We were much amused at his shop. His sons are ingenious young men, and have got a method of binding books in vellum, with drawings in black and white on the sides, like blacklead pencil or indian ink, but which will not rub out. They have great demand for these things, and are perpetually employed by Lady Rockingham, and

---

[1] Mr. Edwards, then a bookseller in Halifax, had for many years an extremely valuable collection of books.

Lady ——, and Lady ——, and all the great folks
in that country.   I have bespoke two Prayer-books,
as specimens, one for my sister, and the other for
Mrs. T., that they may keep pace with the great
ladies of the North.

The next morning we set out for Todmorden.
After a mile or two of rising road, where nothing is
to be seen but behind you, you come to a place
called King Cross, where, turning short to the right,
an immense valley opens to your view, a vast basin
of rich and varied prospect, which by its quantity
alone would be striking, though it were a barren
country ; but it is all wood, water, inclosure, habitation, cultivation, &c.   For some way you travel with
this great living map under you on the left ; then
you come to a more beautiful point of view, where,
turning back, you look along the narrower and richer
vale between Ealand and Halifax—the Calder winding
along, a stone bridge, long hanging woods, &c.   I
marked this as one of the very best views I had seen.
At Hepton Bridge, about eight miles from Halifax,
begins the particular style of country which it was
our principal object to see.   Over Hepton Bridge,
on the top of a monstrous hill, is perched the town
of Heptonstall, the first part of the road up to it
having the appearance of an absolute perpendicular.
Our business was, happily, with the valley.   We
pursued the Calder, close to its side in some places,
to Todmorden.   It is not navigable here, but is re-

duced to the 'purling stream' of poetry ; in some
places very little water ; in some, more ; but everywhere a rocky bottom where the water struggles over
great stones, and every now and then a little fall,
so that you hear the river where you do not see it.
The valley contracts itself ; the hills crowd about
you, rising almost perpendicularly on each side,
wooded from top to bottom, with black, craggy
rocks peeping out here and there ; picturesque little
mills, with their rush of water, close under the woods ;
bridges, some stone, of a single arch, others of wood,
but all exactly such as a painter would have them ;
cottages perched about, some in the road, others close
to the stream, others over your head, in most romantic
and improbable situations, more like stone nests than
houses ; here and there little cross vales opening into
this, paths winding up the woods, craggy roads
losing themselves round the corner of a wood, &c.,
&c. I sicken with vague description ! In short, the
effect it had on me (and Elmsall too) was that of
painted landscapes of the most invented and poetic
kind realised ; and every object, animate or inanimate,
that we saw was of a piece with the surrounding scene,
and they seem to have been placed where they were on
purpose as much as mile-stones and guide-posts are
in vulgar roads ; a man with a pack on his shoulder
and a staff in his hand trudging over a rustic bridge,
or climbing up a winding path through a wood ; men
driving pack horses, or lounging along sideways on

the empty pack saddle—a favourite figure with
painters. These people, Elmsall is sure, are paid so
much a day for their attendance. Near Todmorden
there is a change. The vale opens again , but no
wide views. The high woody crags sink, and the
scene changes to wild tumbled ground, a perpetual
wave of smaller hills, where nature seems to have
abhorred a level as much as, according to some
philosophers, she abhors a vacuum. I never saw
ground so shaken about Everywhere habitations ;
but no two houses, I verily believe, upon the same
level. We arrived at Todmorden, where we dined
upon beefsteaks, which we afterwards found were
boiled with a little gravy, and a great deal of melted
butter poured over them, in a deep pan. We returned
to Halifax at night The same beautiful vale con-
tinues beyond Todmorden ; but the weather grew
bad, we were almost satiated with beauty, and I
somewhat fatigued. I would gladly have climbed
some of the steep hills to have looked down into
the valley ; but alas! my breath would not let me
Next morning, after an amusing lounge at M;
Edwards's (the bookseller), we returned to Ealana
to dinner, took a third deliberate and comfortable
view of the valley from different points and different
elevations, and then returned to Emley The sun
shone, and the view was in all its glory The day
before was cloudy, and showed nothing to advantage.
In this respect we were unlucky. Altogether, how-

ever, it was a delightful little excursion. I had never seen such Arcadian scenes but in poetry or painting. I imagine them to be somewhat in the style of Matlock, which you have seen. What is singular is, that you pass through all this retired scene upon turnpike road almost as good as that between Huntingdon and Cambridge! Look down, you are in this world; look up, you are in another.

Of my other expedition to Studley, &c., I will talk another time; indeed, as you have seen those places, I shall have little to say. I find myself comfortably *soulagé* of the labour of attempting to describe them. When you get home I must have your northern journal; your description will now renew the precise ideas of the places, which the best description of a place unseen cannot do. I shall have the pleasure of seeing all over again, and of seeing how we were struck with the same things. I remember you gave the preference to Hackfall, as I do. But your Continental journal! How I shall gormandise! You asked me if I knew of any reading relative to your tour; and I forgot, I believe, to say no. I have no commands for you, except it be that you would present my particular respects to Mr. Kucklehorn, the organist at Aix-la-Chapelle, if you go thither. I hope you will not omit seeing some of the carillonneurs[1] at their work. (Burney's Journal, i. 15.)

[1] His correspondent did not miss 'seeing' and hearing their celebrated performance at Haerlem and at Mechlin—charge at the former place 'a ducat.'

You may see one at Ghent If you have not an ear to judge of music (I say 'if'), you have an eye to judge of labour. If you chance to think on your poor, untravelled, home-bred, elder brother while you are strutting on the banks of the Rhine, with Cæsar's Commentaries in your hand, do not despise him, but pity him When you write say how long you stay, and whether I shall write again, &c. I shall rejoice to hear from you, and to know you are all as you should be, amused and well. I hope you don't know that the Rhine has the property of trying the fidelity of wives. The Germans used to throw in their children for this experiment : if they swam to shore, the mother was good ; if not, not. Sister, hold Mary fast ! Again, heaven bless you all !—so says Mrs. T., with your affectionate brother,

T. T.

REVISING DR. BURNEY'S MANUSCRIPT —MUSICAL CRITICISMS —DR JOHNSON'S 'LIVES.'

To Dr. Burney.

Colchester, December 8, 1781.

How are your patience-pegs ? Have they held fast, or have they slipped ? I am sorry, my dear friend, that I have been forced to put them to such severe trial ; but I could not possibly be more expeditious. For a week, or nearly, after my removal hither I could do nothing, and since that, all my spare time, *i.e.*, all the time I have had for

reading and writing, has been almost cooped up
into the narrow space of two or three hours in a
morning, and those often broke in upon by visitors,
friendly or busy. Still, however, your MS. would
have been returned much sooner, but for the musical
specimens, which neither your request nor my own
curiosity would suffer me to return unexamined.
You, from long habit, have your ear in your eye, and
can, perhaps, hear all the effect of complicated harmony by reading it. So can I, tolerably, in modern
music, and modern notation ; but in this old church
music, with its clefs, its points, its unobvious contrivances, its equally-distributed melody — that is,
every where and no where—its keyless modulation,
and its discretionary supplement of flats and sharps,
&c.—in this music I can do nothing but at a keyed
instrument ; and even so I cannot with much readiness get through the harmony. It is this slow operation that has chiefly detained your MS. so long. Yet
it has given me no trouble but what has been made
good amends for, by the gratification of my curiosity,
and the pleasure I have always taken in analysing the
compositions of what may be called the harmonious
age of music. I have, formerly, studied that kind of
music with some perseverance—scored motetts, mad-
rigals, &c., with great industry—and even tried to
compose in the style. I was, after this hobby was
jaded, as fond of the cantata style of Scarlatti, Gas-
parini, Lotti, &c, and piqued myself upon finding

my way through all the enharmonic tricks and
equivocations of their recitatives. It was Mr. Gray,
principally, who made me first turn my back upon
all this, by his enthusiastic love of expressive and
passionate music, which it was hardly possible for
me to hear and see him feel without catching some
of his prejudices. For Pergolesi was his darling ; he
had collected a great deal of him and Leo in Italy,
and he lent me his books to copy what I pleased.
This was the bridge over which (throwing bundles of
old prejudices in favour of Corelli, Geminiani, and
Handel into the river) I passed from ancient to
modern music. I let my ears and my feelings carry
me which way they pleased, and soon renounced
what was once my creed—that the Pergolesis and the
Leos had carried vocal music to its utmost perfection,
and that nothing was to be done after them.

Now I venture to think myself free from all
musical prejudice ; and though a man must have
neither ear nor soul who is insensible to the wonderful
improvements in melody, grace, expression, rhythm,
and even harmony itself, in some respects, which have
been going on gradually to the present time, yet I
can still see beauties, of another kind, in the ancient
harmonious style which make me listen to it with
great pleasure. As religious music, I really think we
have had nothing comparable to it since. And more
than that may be said in its praise ; but you have
said it all so well, and in such unison with my own

ideas of the matter, in your apology for this old music, that I can do no more than refer you to yourself—vide Burneium.   As for Master Josquin,[1] I go all lengths with you ; he was an admirable fellow, and I had no conception that such harmony existed near a century before Palestrina.   Surely there is nothing of this last composer superior in richness, sweetness, clearness of harmony, and in-genuity of contrivance to Josquin's Misericordias Domini—is there ?   There is even contrast too, which the moderns think they have all to themselves ; for he throws in passages of beautiful simplicity and stable solemnity in the midst of all his art and complication.   Publish that motett, and I will give you a receipt in full for Josquin, though I care not how many specimens of him you can afford to give us.   But as you say you must be as economical here as you can, I should think that two specimens—the motett of his best style and the unfettered powers of his genius, and the Hosanna of the technical style and his tyrannical mastery over difficulties—would be enough to give an adequate idea of his merit and rank.

Next to Josquin, I fancy I see most genius in Fevin.   You will see that I could find nothing of any sort of consequence to object to.   A great part of my paper and my time (and your time too, I fear) you

[1] Després Josquin, a musical composer, born in Hainault, circa 1458 ; d. 1531.

will find occupied by my observations upon the
specimens. When I had examined them at my
pianoforte, I could not refuse myself the pleasure of
telling you all that struck me, not so much as to
beauties, &c., but with respect to passages of harmony
that appeared to me any way remarkable. I was
surprised and pleased to find those old church com-
posers now and then breaking out of their harness,
and carried by their ear and their genius to hazard
passages that anticipated the bolder harmony of
modern times. In all times, and *dans tous les genres*,
genius has taken these occasional strides, and set
examples that mankind were two or three centuries
in collecting the courage to follow. Your time is
precious, and I am not so unreasonable as to desire
you to take notice of all the stuff I scribble, or answer
all my asks. But in this musical business I should
like to know if I am anywhere wrong in my observations about some particular chords and combinations
that I have mentioned. And pray remember that I
wrote these remarks, not for your satisfaction, but
my own. You are so infinitely more *au fait* in such
things than I can pretend to be, that you will not
suppose me such a puppy as to think of suggesting
anything to you. I am giving you my ideas, and
asking you if they are right or wrong.

I found your MS. prodigiously entertaining, and
I have nothing but approbation and praise to give
you. Your musical criticism upon the specimens,

indications of unusual discords, and the gradual and progressive advances of the art, are among the most valuable parts of your work. I will have not a syllable retrenched here, nor object to as large additions as you please to make. It is your own ground —new ground—unoccupied, useful, entertaining, and is the very marrow of your subject—a most essential part of a history of the art. I was much diverted to see how similarly we were both served by this old ecclesiastical music. In your last letter you told me how it stole upon you as you studied it, after a long intermission perhaps, and, from some prejudices against it, brought you to relish its real beauties and be its apologist. I was served just so. You will see plainly that I was in a pet with Ochingheim, half angry and half pleased with Josquin's monody upon him—much pleased with the Hosanna, and delighted with the Misericordias. It was so long since I had unravelled a piece of complicated Church counterpoint that I met, at first, with nothing but difficulties, and it is scarce possible to be plagued and pleased at the same instant, to cry ' Bravissimo !' and ' The ——— take it !' in the same breath. But as soon as I got a little at my ease, my old relish returned, and, without forgetting how much we have that is better, I could do justice to those particular excellences and beauties which are certainly peculiar to that style, and which we have not, though we have greater of other and higher kinds. But now I must wind up ;

for I have been writing till I am tired, and this letter must and shall go by this post.

.   .   .   .   .   .

I thank you much for sending me those duets I am sorry I cannot in conscience make a good report of them I have tried most of them ; but they are very insipid to me, and they are worse than difficult. They are awkward to execute. They have all the appearance of being composed by a man either knowing little of the instrument, or composing without his fiddle in his hand, or in his mind ; and there is very little pleasing or untrite in his melody or harmony. No one of them left any desire of repetition. To show you that I have no quarrel with Dr. Johnson, I have just bought his 'Lives,' and am delighted with his account of the metaphysical poets in his Cowley, which is all I have yet read. Addio. I salute you all in a bunch. Tell Pacchierotti to sing so loud that I may hear him here.—Yours truly,

T. T.

MISS BURNEY'S 'CECILIA.'
To Dr. Burney.

Fordham, September 18, 1782.

I need not tell you that I gobbled up 'Cecilia' as soon as I could get it from my library. I never knew such a piece of work made with a book in my life ! It has drawn iron tears down cheeks that were never wetted by pity before ; it has made novel-readers of

callous old maiden ladies who have not for years
received pleasure from anything but scandal. Judge,
then, what effect it has had upon the young and the
tender-hearted ! I know two amiable sisters at
Colchester, sensible and accomplished women, who
were found blubbering at such a rate one morning!
The tale had drawn them on till near the hour of
an engagement to dinner, which they were actually
obliged to put off, because there was not time to
recover their red eyes and swelled noses. The person
who caught them in this pathetic pickle was alarmed
at their appearance, and thought of nothing less than
of some domestic calamity As to myself, 'Cecilia'
has done just what she pleased with me. I laughed
and cried (for I am one of the blubberers) when she
bade me. How do I like it ? Much, very much,
indeed—better, I think, than 'Evelina,' on the whole,
though particular parts of that are perhaps equal to
anything in 'Cecilia ;' but it is long since I read
'Evelina,' and therefore I cannot fairly compare them.
I must read it again soon, and then I shall know my
mind better. However, I clearly received more pleasure from this novel. My idea in general agrees
exactly with yours. The characters are untrite, yet
real and natural ; admirably kept up, which was the
more difficult as the shades of distinction between
some of them are nice, yet they never run into each
other. The writing, I think, is an improvement upon
'Evelina;' except here and there, where, I think (and

it has struck others), it is not the better for a little imitation (probably involuntary) of Dr. Johnson Among many great beauties, he certainly has two striking faults : he is occasionally verbose, and sometimes he transposes his words to a degree that our language will hardly bear, and which has the effect of perplexing his meaning. I think I remarked a few places of 'Cecilia' where I was reminded of these peculiarities in Dr J.'s manner, but in general, I sincerely think Miss B. (she is not within hearing, I hope) a charming writer, with great command and variety of language, great ease, and more nerve and muscle than commonly falls to the share of a style apparently easy and unlaboured. Her knowledge of the world, her observation of all the minutest peculiarities of ridiculous character—and above all that solidity of stuff, that plenty of sense and reflection that is scattered through the whole—I do unfeignedly admire. Her tragic powers I still think great, though not greater, than I thought them after reading ' Evelina ;' but her comic appear, I think, to vastly more advantage in 'Cecilia.'

We have a circulating library at Colchester, and the bookseller tells me there is such scrambling for ' Cecilia ' Mrs. T was so much pleased with it that she read it twice in a breath. As soon as she had finished she began again. Who will read our histories of music, and our commentaries upon Aristotle, at this rate ?

NOTES ON THE CHARACTERS IN 'CECILIA.'

To Dr. Burney.

Colchester, November 28, 1782.

Again, I fear, I have sinned in not being able to prevail on myself to send you a short answer to your long, friendly, interesting, and communicative letter. But my time lately has been broken to bits, and lost in the confusion of removal ; you would else have heard from me at least a fortnight sooner. And now, my dear friend, take my heartiest thanks for your letter, and for the kind and friendly detail of domestic matters it contained. I read it with eagerness ; your joys and your sorrows, your disappointments and your hopes, all readily found their proper unisons in my feelings.

Your account of the curious opinions of critics and *beaux esprits* about ' Cecilia ' gratified me much. For my part, I did not say half enough to give you an idea of my particular likings. Charles Fox's verdict about the improbability has some weight, for, after all, how far the prejudice of family will go, who can tell but men of family who feel it ? Of the effects of intoxication, are you or I so competent judges as a drunken porter ? Though I said that Simkins and Hobson seemed sometimes to encroach a little, yet I delight in them as much as you can do. They are admirable pieces of nature ; characters that every soul must recognise, and nobody has drawn. What

I

made me sometimes think their company less pleasant, was the high interest of the scenes which they
interrupt; they are always pleasant, but they are
sometimes pleasant when the mind is too much occupied by suspense to relish their humour. I allude
particularly to the scene at Mrs Belfield's, where
young Delvile surprises his wife. I saw some terrible
bévue was coming on, and, agonised with impatience,
I was too anxious to laugh. Why, I thought I did
see some little feebleness in the winding up ; or
rather, I mean, that the conclusion does not leave
one's mind fully satisfied. It may, indeed, be called
a happy ending, but it does not quite come up·to
poetical justice ; a happier was deserved. If we lay
not down the book with tears in our eyes, at least
they look red, they are not thoroughly wiped. Kill
Cecilia ! the very idea makes me shudder ; I think I
never could have forgiven it. It would have been
impossible for any human creature to have read the
book through.

All you say as to your own sentiments about the
Harrels, Mrs. D. Monckton, &c, is to a tittle my
own idea of the matter. Mr. Meadows is particularly my favourite It is a caricature, but of a real
and common character, that wanted to be exposed
to ridicule, and for that purpose must be caricatured.
It is fair, well-aimed ridicule, and new ; indeed, I
do not recollect one trite character in the whole novel ;
nor, at the same time, one unnatural. I have heard

Albany called improbable, but I deny it; his tale reconciles all to the *vraisemblance.* But let me mention one little portrait of exact nature that struck me and Dr. Forster as admirably hit off—the lawyer from the Egglestones. There are undoubtedly things and characters more striking ; but not in the whole book, nor in any other book, is there a juster piece of natural delineation. If you don't distinctly recollect it, I insist upon your reading it. It is page 244 of the last volume. As to moral reflections, observations, and the tendency of the whole, too much cannot be said of them. If the book does no good, it will be because men are incorrigible. I am now reading it aloud and dramatically to a select little party of friends here, *à bâtons rompus,* about half a volume in an evening. I have yet read only vol. i. I have only made my friends admire and laugh as yet, but I shall soon begin to make them blow their noses ; what will become of them and me in the last vol. I don't know.—Yours,

T. T.

READING AND BUSINESS.—MRS. SIDDONS.—THE
CANT OF THEATRICAL CRITICISM.

To his Brother.

Colchester, December 10, 1782.

Last night I received the Virg. MSS. Thanks again. I was astonished at our voluminosity. I look at these communications with a mixture of pleasure and melancholy ; pleasure from the recollection of pleasure, melancholy from the fear that it is a pleasure past and gone [1] I was glad, however, to see you in your last letter casting somewhat like a wistful eye towards the old friends on your shelves. I have said little about this matter, because I would not tease you, because I know how much business you have had upon your hands, because I know also that if the spring was only held back by force, it would in time restore itself ; if broken, it was not a thing to be repaired. To drag others to one's own particular tastes and pursuits is a sort of persecution. Moreover, it is certainly not a thing of the least consequence whether a man chooses to read in dead languages or not ; if the employment does not answer in point of pleasure, it is not on any other account to be urged, at least upon you But, after all this, we are naturally pleased by coincidence of taste in our friends, and naturally disappointed when it appears to cease

[1] My love of reading was not gone , but my opportunities of reading were at that time much diminished. My brother lamented this. I had more reason to lament it I can only say that, by attending to the claims which I then had upon my attention, I was, I believe, doing my duty. Business prevailed over pleasure —R. T., 1817.

At the early age of sixteen his brother Richard was taken from Eton, on the death of his father, to manage the business in the Strand for his widowed mother, a task which he undertook and carried out with great ability, energy, and success. He brought away from Eton an intense love for classical studies, a taste which his elder brother did not fail to encourage with the utmost sympathy and many valuable directions ; and thenceforward no one knew better than my grandfather how to combine the pleasures and refinements of literature with the active duties of a life of business.—R. T., 1881

or to relax. That you have not time, or rather
leisure, enough to occupy yourself in such pursuits,
would not so much concern me, because this I should
regard as a temporary obstacle. All that has morti-
fied me is the fear lest your inclination itself has suffered a change ; lest, in short, that should be fulfilled
which certain prophetesses foretold—namely, that the
taste was only the hobby of the hour, and would pass
away ; and that should not be fulfilled which was
spoken by a certain prophet—namely, ' that Mr.
Richard Twining had found an amusement that would
last for life.' Now I do confess that this idea would
vex me. Do I entertain it ? I cannot admit it, but it
has sometimes pushed for entrance. I wish now you
would ask yourself, and tell me how the case stands ,
for your expressions have never precisely told me
whether your complaint is want of time, and of that
liberty of mind which such pursuits require, or failure
of inclination ; or, in other words, that such studies
do not give you the pleasure they once did   Thanks
for Mrs. Siddons. I had seen her name in the papers,
but never read a word about her. Nothing makes
me so sick as the cant of theatrical criticism which
now fills the papers. But when you talk, sir, I am
all attention and all faith. Nothing can give me
greater expectation than your account.

I am well, robust, and fit to live in Plato's re-
public, where invalids are illegal. How are you ?
how my sister ? how all ? Our loves all round. I

thank John for his very kind and friendly answer to my letter.—Yours affectionately,

T. T.

ACTORS AND ACTING.—A DEFENCE OF SWIFT.

To his Brother.

Colchester, March 14, 1783.

As to my assisting at Mrs. Siddons' benefit, it is out of the question. Then Tuesday is, or used to be, opera night ; and—but this is a tender point ; I must not shock you—I drank tea with an old-fashioned gentleman last night who insisted that we had never any actress at all equal to Mrs. Oldfield and Mrs. Bracegirdle. I was very near spilling my tea over my best small-clothes. My idea of Booth, Betterton, and all those old players, is that they were somewhat of the kind that Partridge liked so much better than Garrick. 'Anybody might see they were actors.' I suppose you have read 'Tom Jones'? I am sadly afraid you have not read 'Cecilia.' If you have not, I shall abuse you ; if you have, and are not delighted with it—I shall say nothing.

As for——'s indignant defence of Swift, that capital man, who has lately been so unfairly attacked by Harris, Beattie, &c., I honour him ; and were I to meet him in a room full of bishops, I would give him both my hands, and thank him loudly. I deny that Swift's writings have any one bad tendency. I deny that he was a misanthrope ; but he talked about it so much that the world have taken it upon his word. He was a great humourist, and they have taken all he has said of himself as if he were not so. What connection is there between indignation at the vices of mankind, and hatred of mankind ? Oh, commend me to the gentle philanthropists and optimists of these days, who think all well while they are well themselves ! But *basta* ; pray now, agree with me about all this Your hand, your hand, I will have your hand You do love Swift, now don't you ? Ay, ay, I knew it. And yet, can you possibly love an ill-natured man ? No. *Ergo*, Swift was not an ill-natured man. But I must stop.

DR JOHNSON'S 'LIVES.'—CRITICAL REMARKS ON JOHNSON.—' DOGMATIC, BUT NEVER DULL !'

To his Brother.

May 3, 1784

As to Dr. Johnson, we seem to agree well in our likings and dislikings. The best thing in all his book [1] is, in my opinion, his critique upon Cowley, or rather upon what I think he calls the metaphysical style of poetry. Such is that of d'Avenant, of whom I wonder he takes no notice. Johnson's mind is fettered with prejudices civil, poetical, political, religious, and even superstitious As a reasoner he is

---

[1] The *Lives of the Poets*. The first part, here noticed, appeared in March 1779, the work having been completed in 1781.

nothing, He has not the least tincture of the *esprit philosophique* upon any subject. He is not a poet, nor has any taste for what is properly called poetry ; for imagination, enthusiasm, &c. His poetry—I mean what he esteems such—is only good sense put into good metre. He sees no promise of Milton's genius in his juvenile poems. He feels no beauties in Mr. Gray's odes. Did you ever see a more school-boyish criticism than his upon Gray ? What he says about blank verse I abominate. To me, a work of length in the rhymed heroic of Pope, &c., is insufferably monotonous and cloying to the ear. It should be appropriated, I think, to short poems and gay subjects. But I must not indulge myself in entering upon my reasons. I have too much to say upon this head Pope's ' Iliad ' he undoubtedly overrates exceedingly. Great merit must be allowed it; great command and variety of versification, &c. ; but as a translation (*i.e.* as a representation of Homer) it is liable to great objection. Rowe's ' Lucan ' I forget. In general I find my palate in matters of poetry continually at variance with Dr. Johnson's. I don't mean this alone as any proof that he is wrong. But the general taste and feelings of the most poetical people, of the best poets, are against him. I will not allow that a man who slights Akenside, abuses Gray, and mentions with complacence such versifiers as Pomfret, Yalden, Watts, &c., in the list of poets, can have any true poetical taste. He is a man of sense, and has an ear ; that is all. And how he praises Dryden's translations ! Can a translation deserve praise that cannot be read ? That to me is the case with Dryden's ' Virgil.' With all this, Dr. Johnson is always entertaining, never trite or dull. His style is just what you say ; sometimes admirable, sometimes laughable, but he never lets you gape. Without being philosophical or deep, like Hume, Lord Kaimes, &c, he has his originalities of thought, and his own way of seeing things, and making you see them. This is great excellence. There is in him no echo. He is dogmatical certainly, and I cannot acquit him of some reflections that savour of ill-nature —Yours affectionately,

T. T.

WARBURTON AND ADDISON — MILTON'S PROSE —LA FONTAINE —CONDILLAC.

To Dr. Burney.

Colchester, May 6, 1784.

The 'great writer' who called Addison 'an indifferent poet, and a worse critic,' was Warburton, I believe I think it is in his notes on Pope. The first part of the charge is certainly just. The other, methinks, is *outré*. A man of so much taste could not well be a worse than indifferent critic. The truth is, that Mr. Addison had not that philosophical turn of mind that is necessary to the best criticism ; at least to that sort of criticism that consists in analysing the beauties of poetry, tracing them to their sources, and accounting for their effects. He was an excellent popular critic, but a very indifferent philosophical critic. Indeed, he was not a philosopher at all. Among many good things, and much display of taste, in his papers upon the 'Pleasures of Imagination,' you will find a lamentable shallowness in all his attempts to account for things. You, who have read Locke, Hume, Helvetius, &c., will easily perceive this defect in all Addison's writings ; nay, you would undoubtedly have perceived it though you had never read any of those writers, for your mind is of a philosophical mould.

I never saw the answers to Dr. Johnson that you speak of. Potter's I have read, and it gives him some hard blows with great justness. Though Milton's letter to Mr. Hartlib on education is, as you say, impracticable in many respects, yet I never read it without pleasure. The excellence of that man as a prose writer is very little known. His force is wonderful ; and the richness of his fancy often breaks out where one would least expect it. The part about music is to me delightful. The 'Areopagitica' is an old favourite of mine. It is all nerve and sense, manly freedom, elevation of mind ; it is throughout strong, harmonious, and in some places even sublime. One passage, of which I cannot now recollect any of the words, is a perfect model, I think, of fine writing, or rather of excellence. Oh, I have a morsel of it: ' Liberty, which is the muse of all great wits ; this is that which hath rarified and enlightened our spirits like the influence of heaven ; this is that which has enfranchised, enlarged, and lifted up our apprehensions,' &c.   Read on—his address to the Legislature is fine, &c.   Above all, read this whole tirade aloud, and conceive yourself speaking to a great assembly, for it is something beyond writing.   And mark how full and round and satisfying it is to the ear.   I once had this by heart, and I remember spouting it aloud in Twickenham Park to my father and Sir John Hawkins.   If you are not pleased with this passage in his tract on Education, I shall wonder :—' In these vernal seasons of the year, when the air is calm and pleasant, it were an injury and sullenness against nature not to go out and see her riches, and partake in her rejoicing with heaven and earth.'

Phædrus is elegant undoubtedly, but no more to be compared to La Fontaine! The beauty of Phædrus seems to be chiefly in his language, in his Latinity ; a beauty of which we are, after all, but incompetent judges.   In the French fabulist there is a grace, a humour, a *naïveté*, that is totally wanting in Phædrus. Totally may be rather too much, but it seems very near the truth.   I never read d'Alembert's Jesuit work ; it is not printed in his ' Mélanges,' &c., which I have, and which are well worth your having.   He is a charming writer, elegant and philosophical ; and always clear and neat.   If you have not his ' Mélanges ' (5 tom.) by all means get them.   You ask me if I

have anything in the metaphysical way to recommend
to you.   Yes ; I recommend Condillac's ' Essai sur
l'Origine des Connaissances Humaines,' two little
volumes.   I read it with much pleasure a few years
ago ; have since bought it, and mean to read it again.
I thought it excellent, but who expects to be satisfied
with everything in any book ?   He is, I think, the
first—*i.e.* the best— of French metaphysicians.   But I
will not forestall.   So much for odds and ends.

GILPIN'S TOURS.

To Dr. Burney.

Fordham, September 18, 1784.

That delightful little book of Mr. Gilpin's about
the Wye gives me the highest idea of his taste.   It
is not the loose, shambling gusto of a mere con-
noisseur, a man that only knows he is pleased or dis-
pleased, but does not know why ; it is exact, precise,
philosophical taste, that supposes much experience,
comparison, and reflection.

They tell me, by the way, that Mr. Gilpin intends
to publish his other journals, of the Lakes, &c., by
subscription.   I hope it is true.   I will subscribe to
them all, though I subscribe myself into the work-
house.   And how you have made my mouth water
with your account of your nephew's drawings !   Sir, I
am absolutely '*fou de ces choses-là.*'   I may say, as
old Richardson did of poetry, if music is my wife,

painting is my concubine. I hope those engravings will do your nephew great credit, and give him a good shove forward. I have seen some of his works, particularly a portrait of, I think, your poor friend Mr. Crisp, of great force and nature. *Et puis*—the Worcester family-piece of your performance—nothing could be so tempting to me ; but I have dropped all thoughts of so distant an excursion at this time of the year. I must, however, thank you heartily for the satisfactory and pleasant account you give me of 'them there people.' Talk of ploughing waste lands, enclosing commons, and a parcel of stuff ; were I a member of the House of Commons I would bring in a Bill for procuring slips of Burney's, and setting them in every county in England, Wales, and the town of Berwick-upon-Tweed. What an improvement ! Here I am sorry I must stop, but the horse is in the chaise for Colchester. I will hope to see you soon, but you shall hope nothing.—Yours ever,

T. T.

COMPLETION OF THE 'HISTORY OF MUSIC.'—THE DEATH OF DR. JOHNSON.

From Dr. Burney to the Rev. T. Twining.

Christmas Day, 1784.

Ah ! my ever dear friend, that I should be fated to let the sweetest and most gratifying letter I ever received from you remain, *invita Minerva*, so long unanswered ! We have nothing to do with free will,

I'll maintain it ; all our actions have been predestined, from eternity, else would not I instantly have told you that I had thought you a 'leetle' naughty, and the time betwixt your departure and my receipt of your letter a great while ; but that your hand instantly wiped away all naughtiness from the score between us, and so far from its seeming a great while since I saw you, this same letter brought you so full to my view that I was ready to swear you were present during the perusal of it, and to knock any one down who should dare to prove an *alibi*. Day after day, week after week, month after month have I expected to be able to present my Commemoration Account to you and to his Majesty, and though my Epistle Dedicatory to you is not yet written, that to his Majesty has been printed more than a month, and all the letterpress of my book ready for binding ; but engravers and other *diavolacci degl' impedimenti* swore bloodily it should not appear till next year. What bitter histories I could give you of unforeseen plagues in this business, besides those which from the beginning stared me full in the face ! I shall only say, in few, that besides the disappointments of engravers, the grateful Musical Society for whom I have been royally commanded to write have as yet taken no proper measures for defraying the expenses of printing, paper, and plates, so that unless I redeem the sheets and plates, when finished, with my own credit and purse, the book will remain some time unpublished for want of money to pay the artists that have been employed.

The next subject of my scribble shall be your *protégé*, the painter. If any possible means of serving such a man as you describe had occurred to me on or since the perusal of your letter you would certainly have heard from me sooner ; but, alas ! I have long seen and predicted that the polite arts have been fostered, cherished, and are arrived almost at maturity in this ruined country merely to be starved to death ! The swarm of young artists who have been students in the Royal Academy has over-stocked the capital and country so much that I am told many of them are at present in the utmost indigence. Zoffani and Humphreys are gone to the East Indies, and Pine, with several others, to the West. It is the same with music ; many masters, once in great business, are now wholly scholarless, without any other cause assigned but the general declension of the kingdom. Schools are indeed multiplied ; but their existence is of short duration. The governesses, beginning on credit and a little money borrowed at very exorbitant interest, never subsist above three or four years, running in debt with every one that will trust them, and then suddenly disappearing. The poor masters are certain sufferers on these occasions. I have felt their bankruptcies a little ; but Mr. Burney very heavily. To such unestablished schools as these I should be sorry to recommend your friend ; and to others of long

standing the masters are generally of the highest
rank in their profession.   A man who has a name to
make, whatever his intrinsic worth and abilities, will
never get into a great school but as an assistant.
After this gloomy description of the general state
of the arts and their votaries in London, you may
be assured, my dear friend, that any person recommended by you can never be out of my thoughts,
and if anything should offer within my ken and
power of influence it shall be instantly communi-
cated to you.   Poor Fisin, who has always done your
patronage credit, seems to find it more and more
difficult to subsist in London, and is languishing
for a quiet organist's place in the country.   I tried
to get Newcastle for him some years ago, but was
foiled.   He was not, however, rejected for want of
splendid abilities, as might naturally be expected ;
but for want of friends powerful enough to overset
the natural interest of a man in the neighbourhood,
not much his superior in talents, and greatly his
inferior in good qualities.

Poor Johnson is gone !   I truly reverenced his
genius, learning, and piety, without being blind to
his prejudices.   I think I know and could name
them all.   We often differed in matters of taste,
and in our judgments of individuals   My respect for
what I thought excellent in him never operated on
my reason sufficiently to incline me to subscribe to
his decisions when I thought them erroneous.   The

knight, Sir John [Hawkins], and I met two or three times during his sickness, and at his funeral. He steps forth as one of poor Johnson's six or eight biographers, with as little taste or powers of writing worthy of such an occupation as for musical history. The Dean and Chapter of Westminster Abbey lay all the blame on him for suffering Johnson to be so unworthily interred. The knight's first inquiry at the Abbey, in giving orders, as the most acting executor, was—'What would be the difference in the expense between a public and private funeral?' and was told only a few pounds to the prebendaries, and about ninety pairs of gloves to the choir and attendants; and he then determined that, 'as Dr. Johnson had no music in him, he should choose the cheapest manner of interment.' And for this reason there was no organ heard, or burial service sung; for which he suffers the Dean and Chapter to be abused in all the newspapers, and joins in their abuse when the subject is mentioned in conversation. Dr. Bell has stated the case, in a letter to my friend Dr. Warren, just as I tell it you. Again, I was told by a lady 'that she found Dr. Johnson had not been always so pious and good a Christian as in the latter part of his life.' 'How do you know, madam?' 'Why, Sir John Cullum was told so by Sir John Hawkins, who says that when Dr. Johnson came up to London first he lived a very profligate life with Savage and others, and was an infidel, and that he (Hawkins) first

K

converted him to Christianity!' This astonished me
so much that I could not help mentioning the story,
and my authority, to Johnson's oldest and most intimate friends, with whom I dined after attending the
funeral to Westminster Abbey, and asked them if
ever they heard of Johnson having been a profligate
and an infidel in his younger days, and they one
and all cried out, with astonishment and indignation,
'No!' Dr. Scott, one of the three executors, said
that he had found among his papers a great number
of prayers, penned with great force, elegance, and
devotion, some of them as high up as the year 1738,
which would be a sufficient answer to such a charge;
and I hear to-day that Dr. Scott, without mentioning
names, has said to the knight that such a report had
got about. 'Oh!' says Sir John, 'I can best confute
such a rumour, who have so long known him, and
ever found him a man of the most exemplary life,
and a most steady believer of the doctrines of the
Christian religion.' This strange story, for the honour
of Johnson and true piety, as well as the clearing up
the point which now lies between the reverend and
irreverend knight, I hope and trust will be sifted to
the bottom. I shall write again in my book parcel as
soon as his Majesty is 'sarved,' and then tell you the
upshot. What an excellent writer and speaker is
your (my) brother-chairman become in a short time!
'Oh! most righteous judge! A second Daniel!' I
wish I had leisure to follow him to the India House;

but, alas! there would soon be a 'sale' at mine if I did !

A pit of destruction for the man who robbed us, in one year, of so many comforts ! and, among the rest, of the power of tiring our friends to death with frequent and long letters, *à bon marché*! Why, now I am but just got into my rate, and am obliged to pull up ! I have lately had very pleasant accounts from (the) Philippi, where I should like to meet you next summer. I have not been able to bestow a thought on my poor History, or the idea of a design for a frontispiece (which you do me the honour to remember better than myself), since I saw you. Indeed, I once tried to find the sketch I read to you, in order to show it to Sir Joshua Reynolds, but could not. Shrocter's second book of concertos has more nerves than the first, and the parts of both are well written and adjusted ; but, I know not how it is, I tire of both very soon. I have not yet been at the opera. There is nothing new in the comic line ; and Cherubini, the second composer, with Crescentini, the first serious man, and the Ferrarese, the first woman, being all principiants, I have no more desire to dress and go into the cold theatre to hear them than to go to a puppet-show, or to see the giants at Guildhall. Lolli, the great violinist, is just arrived. Addio.

C B.

MUSICAL CRITICISMS.—WARREN HASTINGS AND
PARTY SPIRIT.

To Dr. Burney.

Colchester, March 27, 1786.

—— runs down harmony because (I know, and
have known many years) he is not harmonist enough
to relish it.   No man likes what he does not understand.   A man who has not habituated his mind to the
close attention that strict reasoning requires, takes up
Locke or Hume, and soon throws them aside as bores.
I suppose the ' Bow thine ear ' of Bird is all confusion
in Mr. ——'s ear ; he has not made himself a harmonic
ear, or perhaps nature has not given him one   But see
how he admires the tautological sing-song of Marcello's
' O Lord ! our Governor,' &c. !   But I contend that the
whole foundation of his criticism is a chimera—*i.e.*
that vocal music and vocal performance are good
for nothing if the words are not perfectly intelligible
to the hearer without the assistance of his eyes or
memory.   Won't you join with me in absolutely
denying this ?   It seems to me much nearer the
truth to say that when the words are perfectly
distinct, as in reading, it must be a proof that the
music or the singer, or both, are bad.   I have heard
Beard commended for this.   But was that singing ?
Did not syllable swallow up note ?   All this is un-
musical criticism, and goes upon the false notion of
the words, or poetry, being principal.   From the

very nature of music, as a high sensible pleasure (for sensual is ambiguous), it always will and must be principal in the union with words, whatever may be determined as to the separate claims of poetry and music to superiority   But do we not carry prayer-books to church to read even while the minister is reading ?   Are there not anthem books in all cathedrals?   Who can understand even the common Psalms, when sung or chanted to the simplest music, without the assistance of a book ?   I never could. Mr. —— says that ' singers should endeavour to hit that precise medium in the vocal faculty which pronounces and sings at the same time, and which is at once, in point of sound, melodious, and in point of speech, articulate.'   Now, I say there exists no such medium.   What say you? . . .   It will be an excellent article, and of most righteous judgment. I am in a fit of entire callosity about him just now, because he asserted the other day (but not in my hearing ; if he had, I should have contradicted him at right angles) that Jommelli never composed anything worth a farthing.   All he ever heard of Jommelli, I believe, is the overture in E Flat, where, however, there is a *chaconne* worth many farthings and many fugues.   Ay, my curate, now, is another guess-sort of a dilettante.   He has sent me, at my request, copies of some of his things, particularly a song (as he calls it) from the 5th Psalm, ' I will lay me down,' &c, accompanied by a fiddle, tenor, and a

viola obbligata, that is really excellent, and, as far as
I can judge, would disgrace no professor. As for
novelty, refinement, and those bold and, as it were,
prophetic stretches of invention that outstrip the
age, all this, you know, is to be expected only from
your E. Bachs, your Haydns, &c. . . . As for
Mr. Hastings,[1] I am all suspense and candour. I
believe there is much truth in your account of the
matter How I detest the thing called party !

AN IMAGINARY VISIT TO PARIS

To his Brother.

Fordham, August 27, 1786.

As you wished to hear from me during your pere-
grination, you see I lose no time, for I received
your letter but yesterday. Where mine will find you,
the god of travelling (if there is such a heathen god-
likin) only knows. I shoot at you flying. I fear it
will not catch you at Paris *N'importe.* But are you
really, were you really, at Paris ? It seemed an impo-
sition when I read your letter. The hand, the paper, the
folding up, were exactly as if it came from Devereux
Court And why not ? nay, I know not ; but I expect nothing that comes from abroad to look like
anything here. But, *eh bien, chers amis,* how do ye
do ?—*touchez, touchez,* I am *ravi* to meet you at

---

[1] The trial of Warren Hastings.

Paris.¹   Hurri, hurri—z—s ! the cabriolet will be
over us Sir, I am *bien obligé* for your information,
but I believe I am pretty well *au fait* of everything
at Paris. Have they pulled down those vile old
buildings yet upon the Pont St. Michel and Pont
au Change? They terribly obstruct the view from
the Pont Royal, which I think is very fine, or would
be if the Seine were a little less ditchy. Yes ; Paris
abounds with fine buildings, if there were but a place
to see them from. Notre Dame is fine and venerable,
but not so light, I think, as Westminster Abbey.
The range of pictures within have to me a rich and
striking appearance.   But is not the façade of St.
Geneviève fine ?

But let me, at last, have the grace to thank you
for writing to me. I really did not expect it, knowing full well how precious every moment is to a man
in your situation, and conscious that were I at Paris
I should, I verily believe, find no time to write to
any soul but Mrs. T. It was a great treat to me to
find your letters upon Mrs. T.'s table yesterday; and
more, of course, to open and to read them. Why,
I always supposed and understood that one might
be free and easy and please one's self at Paris. Else
why the proverbial expression of 'taking a French
leave'? M. Le Mercier has said so much about the

---

¹ My brother had never been abroad, but he had just been reading
M. Peltier's *Tableau de Paris*, and he was much pleased with it.—
R. T., 1818.

inhumanity of the cabriolet gentry to the poor Pictons, that I almost wonder he has not produced a little degree of reformation ; an effect which, I understand, his book has had in some respects. As to pictures, though I verily believe I love painting as much as you do, yet I think I should not in your place lament the ill-luck you talk of so much as you seem to do.[1] Ill-luck it certainly is, however ; but all I mean is, that were I at Paris, I should not like to bestow much of my time upon seeing pictures. Many objects would press upon my curiosity before that. My two great objects would be place and people, including in the idea of place, buildings, streets, every local pecu- liarity, everything that is Paris and is not London ; everything that would send me home with a good lasting impression of the place in my sensorium ; and in people, including everything I could get at by con- versation with high and low as they came in my way ; everything that would furnish me with a tolerable picture of that great collective mass, the French nation.' But you will think me mighty wise and sententious. I have another idea (for I find I must go on). If I were to go to Paris, I should not wish to see the face of any English creature, except my *compagnons de voyage,* all the time I was there. I should wish to be in French company. But I know this is not always feasible. One must have good letters of recommendation. But it is always in one's

[1] The Luxembourg Gallery was closed.

power to talk with the lower sorts of people, and I certainly should take every opportunity of doing it. I would let a Savoyard clean my shoes upon the Pont Neuf, on purpose to hear him talk, &c. In short, the peculiarities of national character, manners. and language—these to me would be the great charm of travelling. Last, all those things that we may see as well in other places, and at home ; though not the individual things (for to be sure a picture or a prospect cannot be in two places at once), yet things of the same kind, and as good. And so ends my sapient sermon (it is my preaching day, you know) upon the true use of one's eyes in foreign countries.

But pray see Le Sueur's St Bruno ; that comes under my localities. Ay, and I am very sorry the Luxembourg Gallery is shut up. Peste ! the fellows will spoil all the pictures, but I suppose you would be sent to the Bastille if you should say so. Yes, my brother was so good as to send me his map ; but I took it only as a loan It has gratified my curiosity much. You say nothing of the Boulevards. They must be pleasant and amusing. It seems to me that Paris has an advantage over London in the circumstance of being divided by its river. At least it must produce a variety in the Paris walking and riding, which the London walking and riding has not. A river, even though not a good one, is always a pleasant scene How I envy you the spectacles of Paris. My idea is that the French outdo us in comedy ; that they are

more easy, natural, and real. But I hope you will see
a tragedy. It would be a great object of curiosity to
me to hear and see a tragedy of Corneille, Racine,
or Voltaire. I don't know what kind of thing their
declamation is. I should rather expect to dislike it
What! did not you know that Arlequin spoke French!
Fi donc! I have known that, sir, time out of mind.
By the accounts I have had of the Comédie Italienne,
it is a sort of folly that would make me laugh heartily;
but perhaps what you saw was only a singing comedy,
for such, I think, are performed at that theatre. Oh,
I have a very mean idea of the concert spiritual.
Indeed, no man must go from England to France to
hear music. I hope, however, you will see one serious
opera, for I believe it is quite unlike what is to be
seen and heard anywhere else. If the French do not
prize Diderot, *tant pis pour eux*; and you may tell
them so from me ; but I mean merely as a writer, for
I know no more of him. I desire you to make two
very important enquiries for me. I want very much
to know what a '*Perruque à trois Marteaux*' is, which
Le Mercier says, '*frappe singulièrement tous les
étrangers*,' and so note it well, for I hope it is something
very ridiculous. (A man with such a wig, &c., is described in the 'Tableau de Paris,' vol. v, ch. 401.)
Next, what is, or was, a Calambour? Le Mercier talks
of it as some whimsical and fashionable perversion of
language, but what it is I can't make out. I hope
you have contemplated the Bastille, and the bone-

breaking Place de Grève, with the pleasurable horror of a man who is conscious that he is not likely to be imprisoned in the one, or to have his legs and arms smashed with an iron bar in the other.

LORD CHESTERFIELD'S LETTERS TO HIS SON.

To Dr. Burney.

Now I talk of letters, I declare to you I can't bear Lord Chesterfield's, that are so puffed off. He makes me sick with his graces and manners, &c., &c. He would have been shocked, I suppose, to have been called pedant ; but his letters are full of the most offensive of all pedantry, *selon moi*—the pedantry of gentlemanship. Good breeding is a very good thing ; but two quartos about good breeding ! And what pages of trite, trifling stuff for now and then a little wit ! His immoral advice is worse still. One may dislike that, I think, not as '*homme de Dieu*,' but as '*homme d'homme*.'

THE PROJECTED EDITION OF ARISTOTLE.

To Dr. Burney.

Fordham, October 19, 1786

What you say about procrastination and age stealing on, and the feeling of being busied about what one may never finish, and of sacrificing 'good days that might be better spent' to—I know not what; how I, too, have felt all this. I have about ten years less upon my head than you have ; yet I assure you I have been, and am, perpetually haunted with that whisper you talk of, 'Make haste, or you will be too late!' I have always said—as I love, you know, like Vellum, to be jocose—that it was a moot point whether my work or my teeth would be out first. But what of all this ? let us not croak, nor repent of our undertakings. As long as my pursuits have amused me, I have been content ; when I have been tired or disgusted, I have stopped. I have not thought of my work for months together ; yet the idea of having given so much time and pains to it, and then burning my papers, has vexed me, and has goaded me on when the fit of industry has returned. Lately I have got on so far, that I do now believe I may be ready for the press by the winter after this next. Yet the very word press makes me shudder. I have a terrible idea of that same public ; and, honestly speaking, without affectation, no high idea of my work, or the importance of it. The extreme depravation of the text, and its obscurities and ambiguities, are such that I have been forced to give up a greater portion of my comment to philological disquisitions than I could have wished ; and a great part of my pains have been employed in proving passages to be unintelligible. But what then ? when people fancy they understand what they do not, it is doing some good to show them that they do not. It is of some use to pull down what is wrong, if one can't build up what is right. I have played Pleyel lately, as Fisin can tell you, and liked him much.

A BOOK WITHOUT AN INDEX.—DR. JOHNSON'S IDEAS OF POETRY.

To Dr. Burney.

Fordham, August, 1788.

I hate a book without an index. How perpetually have I been plagued with hunting for something I had read and liked, but knew not where to find, and could not find at all, though certain of its being somewhere in the book! As for preface, it is not yet fabricated, or rather not finished; for I have made a sort of a *sbozzo*, somewhat like such a landscape as rain makes upon an old wall, or coffee leaves behind it in a cup. I never set about any task so *à contraggenio*. As to Dr. J[ohnson] I fear I have lost all my credit with you by my stroke at his 'Anti-Grayism,' p. 385-6. But I should have burst if I had not spoken my mind about 'that there' But you see I am not an anti-Johnsonian. Heaven forbid! I honour him, and admire him, and have sufficiently shown that I do by quotations from him, and other mention of him. In his ideas of poetry I hold him to have been both *borné* and prejudiced. Is it credible that he should scout Gray's Bard, and yet pronounce Dryden's ode upon the death of Ann Killigrew to be 'undoubtedly the noblest ode that our language has ever produced'!

SIR JOSHUA REYNOLDS IN OLD AGE

To his Brother.

Fordham, October 9, 1789.

I beg your pardon for an unpardonable piece of *étourderie* I committed last Saturday. I carried my letter to Colchester, to put it into the post, and brought it home again in my pocket, and have had no opportunity of conveying it to the post during this vile week. Well, you must have two letters at once from me, as I have had from you.

Why, what excellent company you are in a sale-room![1] I hope Mr. —— overlooked you that day. But where did you pick up that curious letter? Did you compose it *sur le champ*, or copy it? It was impossible you could remember it. You, it seems, have read Paley. I have not, so that I can say nothing as to his moral principle. But what you say in general seems very true. As to my friend the Professor,[2] methinks I shall be sorry if he quits Gottingen. As to your scruples, there does seem something shabby in trying to tempt him away; and yet I am not clear that the two cases of an university and an individual are exactly alike, or rather, I am clear that they are

[1] The East India Company's sale room at the quarterly tea sales was a scene of such incredible uproar and (to any stranger) dire confusion, as might well make it a wonder that any one could undertake letter writing therein, not to mention the intense pressure of work upon those who were interested in the sale.—R T., 1881

[2] Professor Heyne, a correspondent of Thomas Twining.

not exactly alike. This I am sure of, however, that the Professor cannot be censured for accepting a very advantageous offer, if it is made him.

Thanks as to my house. But who is your friend the Consul?[1] Not 'Consul unius anni,' I hope, if he gets into my house. Good night. My hand aches. I suppose the Dr. has written to you ere this.

Remember us to mother, love to sister, &c.— Yours affectionately, T. T.

Poor Sir Joshua Reynolds! I have a sad account of him from Dr. Burney, who went lately to see him. One eye entirely gone, as he told Dr. B. himself; the other cannot bear the light. He will never take the pencil again. He is calm and cheerful. His niece, Miss Palmer,[2] reads to him; and when he is not listening, he amuses himself with dusting his pictures and changing their places. Alas! alas!

MUSICAL GOSSIP.—HAYDN'S WORKS.—DR. PRIESTLEY'S ANSWER TO BURKE.

To Dr. Burney.

Colchester, February 15, 1791.

. . . And now, my dear friend, let's draw our stools together, and have some fun. Is it

---

[1] 'The Consul,' Consul Davison, previously British Consul at Algiers. He became the tenant of Dial House, Twickenham.

[2] 'Miss Palmer,' afterwards Marchioness of Thomond. It is mentioned in another letter that she read as much of 'the Aristotle' as she was able to Sir Joshua.

possible we can help talking of Haydn first?
How do you like him? What does he say? What
does he do? What does he play upon? How
does he play? . . . The papers say he has been
bowed to by whole orchestras when he has appeared
at the play-houses. Is he about anything in the way
of composition? Come! come! I'll pester you no
more with interrogations; but trust to your generosity
to gratify my ardent curiosity in your own way. I
have just—and, I am ashamed to say, but just—sent
for his 'Stabat Mater.' Fisin told me some quartetts
had, not long ago, been published by him. He has
written so much that I cannot help fearing he will
soon have written himself dry. If the resources of
any human composer could be inexhaustible, I should
suppose Haydn's would ; but as, after all, he is but a
mortal, I am afraid he must soon get to the bottom
of his genius-box. How does Girovetz go on? That
man seems to me to have a something of his own
mixed with the improvement which every man must
owe to his predecessors in the art. I look upon it to
be, at this time of day, the most difficult thing of all
in music to produce a piece of melody that shall seem
to be new, without being forced and queer. Now, I
think I hear such little bits of felicity, every now and
then, in Girovetz's air. I know it would be a bold thing
to assert of any melodious phrase that it is absolutely
new, and has never been produced before ; but musical novelty is not to be taken in so strict a sense. We

may fairly call a passage new when it strikes an ear
hackneyed in good melody as, on the whole, uncommonly pleasing *N'est-ce pas ?*

We have lately had very comfortable fiddling
here, indeed, the best dilettante fiddling I ever had
to do with. My friend Mr. Tindal is come to settle
(for the present, at least) in this neighbourhood. He
is going to succeed me in the curacy of Fordham.
He plays the fiddle well, the harpsichord well, the
violoncello well. Now, sir, when I say 'well,' I can't
be supposed to mean the wellness that one should
predicate of a professor who makes those instruments
his study ; but that he plays in a very ungentleman-
like manner, exactly in tune and time, with taste,
accent, and meaning, and the true sense of what he
plays, and, upon the violoncello, he has execution
sufficient to play Boccherini's quintettos at least
what may be called very decently. But ask Fisin ;
he will tell you about our fiddlings, and vouch
for our decency, at least. I saw in one of the
public prints an insinuation that Haydn, upon his
arrival in London, had detected some forgeries,
some things published in his name that were not
done by him. Is that true ? It does not seem very
unlikely.

Have you read Dr Priestley's answer to Mr.
Burke ? [1] If you have, tell me how it worked with

[1] Referring to Dr. Priestley's ' Letters ' to Burke, in which he justified
the French Revolution against Burke's strictures. Published in London, 1791.

you. A friend of mine, a very sensible man, who was much delighted with Mr. Burke's book, says that Dr Priestley's pamphlet has, 'in some respects, rather pulled down Mr. Burke a little in his idea.' I have not read Priestley's book yet; but I intend to read it. Mr. Burke's eloquence runs away with me while I am reading him ; but I felt, sometimes, as if some things were pushed too far, and as if it was possible that he might be mistaken in some facts. Take it, however, all together, I believe I shall always think it a capital performance, and right, solid, and irrefragable in the main ; and considered as an occasional book, meant to oppose and disgrace the wild and dangerous principles of modern reformers, revolutionists, and triers of confusion.

Well, here I am at the end of my paper, and I seem not to have half done with you. I do hope 'Metastasio' by this time has one foot in the press (marry, a scurvy comparison that of a press to a grave). . . . I, too, am put to my shifts, though my books do not breed so fast as yours By the way, I believe I must get Alison's book on Taste, &c. It seems by the extracts in the 'Monthly Review' to be a superior kind of thing in its way. What's your notion ? Do gratify me ere long with Haydn news, opera news, C. B. news, &c. Addio.—Yours ever,

T. T.

HAYDN IN LONDON.—A 'SWEET STRADUARIUS.'

To Dr. Burney.

Colchester, May 4, 1791.

How good it was of you to gratify me with another canto of the 'Haydniad'! It is all most interesting to me. I don't know anything—any musical thing—that would delight me so much as to meet him in a snug quartett party, and hear his manner of playing his own music. If you can bring about such a thing while I am in town, either at Chelsea or at Mr. Burney's, or at Mr. Salomon's, or at I care not where, if it were even in the black hole at Calcutta (if it is a good hole for music)—I say, if by hook or by crook you could manage such a thing, you should be my Magnus Apollo for the rest of your life. I mention Salomon because we are a little acquainted. He has twice asked me to call upon him, and I certainly will do it when I come to town. I want to hear more of his playing ; and I seem, from the little I have seen of him, to like the man. I know not how it is, but I really receive more musical pleasure from such private *cameranious* fidd-lings, and singings, and keyed instrument playings than from all the *apprêt* of public and crowded per-formances. But how mad it made me to think that all that good music you tell me of, and Haydn's original fiddling, and the exquisite expression of his ' Passione,' should be spilt into the unworthy and leathern ears of that raw, staring, schoolboy-faced simpleton ——

That was cutting a block with a razor I am sure. If Haydn had known as much of him as I do, he never could have answered it to his conscience even to try to give him so much pleasure. But I am envious, you see, and you must allow for that. But how provoking that I should get the wrong cantata ! and yet there is no wrong in the matter, for I suppose it is Haydn's; and it is charming, I think, be it whose it will I will try again

I am sorry you think I undervalue the Stabat. I allow the merit of quitting his instrumental eccentricity, and getting into the right style ; still from him I should have expected more novelty in that style. Some of his movements are certainly fine. Others appeared to me common, and somewhat *passés*. The concluding fugue, in particular, I thought not good in its *genre* ; far below such movements in Jommelli, in Pergolesi's Masses, &c. Yes, yes ; you hitched your names cleverly enough into rhyme. I found no fault with your dexterity. But I am almost sure that if you were to read your own verses out to anybody, you would somehow feel yourself bobbing down below poetry when you came to those lines. You would feel them dry, prosaic, and cataloguish, and be glad when you had got through them, and felt yourself buoying up again to the right level. The propriety of the names I am far from meaning to dispute. And if it was necessary to group them in verse, it could not be done better.

I have lately had a sort of fiddle mania upon me, brought on by trying and comparing different Stainer's, Cremona's, &c. I believe I have got possession of a sweet Straduarius, which I play upon with much more pleasure than my Stainer ; partly because the tone is sweeter, mellower, rounder, and partly because the stop is longer. My Stainer is undersized ; and on that account less valuable, though the tone is as bright, piercing, and full, as of any Stainer I ever heard. Yet when I take it up after the Straduarius, it sets my teeth on edge. The tone comes out plump, all at once. There is a comfortable reserve of tone in the Straduarius, and it bears pressure, and you may draw upon it for almost as much tone as you please. I think I shall bring it to town with me, and then you shall hear it. 'Tis a battered, shattered, cracky, resinous old blackguard. But if every bow that ever crossed its strings from its birth had been sugared instead of resined, more sweetness could not come out of its belly. Addio, and ever pardon my sins of infirmity.—Yours truly,

T. T.

LOUIS XVI. AND THE REVOLUTION.

To his Brother.

Colchester, July 7, 1791.

I have felt, and do feel with you, about these poor imprisoned and degraded kings and queens. Devoutly did I wish the king to have escaped,[1] and I could scarce have thought that anything not closely touching me could have vexed me so much as I was vexed by his capture. The whole affair has amazingly occupied and filled my mind ; perhaps were I to be cool enough to philosophise about it, I should hardly know why. Without philosophising, I know very well that a king is but a man ; still I cannot yet shake off old prejudices as not to feel for what concerns a king more, or rather, perhaps, differently, from what I should feel for a cobbler or a butcher. I am afraid what Mr. Hume says (as I remember) is very true, that 'it is but a foolish wisdom, which is so carefully displayed in undervaluing princes, and placing them on a level with the meanest of mankind.' (See his essay on the ' Protestant Succession.' I remembered only the passage in general, and the expression ' foolish wisdom ; ' but turned to the book for the rest. This I put in lest I should seem to pretend to quote the words by memory, a thing I could never do beyond a few words.) There is good sense in the passage. I must do the National Assembly and the people the justice to own that they have behaved better on this occasion than I expected. Yet I think I see there will be dissensions amongst them, and that the king has still friends, perhaps even in the Assembly. I do not know what to say to the king's declaration. One could not expect it to be otherwise than equivocal

[1] The flight of Louis XVI. to Varennes.

and guarded. I do not see but that his declaration about 'not going out of the kingdom' may be consistent with his intention of joining his party, &c. It does not seem necessary for that purpose that he should do more than go to a fortified place near them upon the frontiers. What he says about resisting invasion puzzles me most. Well, it is a sad business, and can never end quietly. I must feel for his miserable state of humiliation and hopeless imprisonment; for so now, I suppose, it is. The party for the king, and the feelings for the king, may be more than they appear to be, for they must necessarily at present conceal themselves. It is dangerous now to express any pity for the king and queen.

THE FRENCH REVOLUTION.—COWPER'S 'HOMER.'

To his Brother.

Colchester, November 29, 1791.

This letter, I calculate, will find you returned from Bitteswell; if not, it will wait patiently a little longer. I shall be heartily glad to hear that you left all well there, or in a good way to be well. As to your silence, I was very glad when it ceased. I can very easily conceive a man to be silent upon his travels; I have often made my confessions to you that I hate letter-writing when I am away from home. But as you are a better sort of man, and have used me to expect letters from you written upon the pommel of

your saddle as you are trotting from place to place,
I did somewhat wonder (but nothing grumble!) that
I heard nothing of you from the Welsh mountains.
You did very well, however, not to waste time, so
precious and so short. I hope you got good as well
as pleasure from the ramble, and that the having been
accessory to the death of a cat will not sit so heavy
upon your conscience as to spoil the pleasure of your
recollections. If you were sorry for the cat, I should
have been sorry too for the hedgehog. Perhaps you
have not the tenderness for hedgehogs that I have.
My little dogs used to put them up now and then in
the wood at Fordham, and by that means I scraped
acquaintance with the animal ; and as I believe they
do no harm, I always took great care of them, and
restored them to the wood unhurt. An enthusiastic
lover of the country as I am is a sort of hedgehog.
Then I am '*hérissé de Grec,*' you know, as Boileau
says of a pedant.

But let us proceed, for I have many things to say
to you. Indeed, the last cartload of French newspapers almost overset my constancy. They are
really too voluminous, and take up too much time
to read, even for me. As for you and my brother
John, I don't see how you can find time even to
skim over them. Yet they are interesting and amusing to me, and I cannot help reading almost the
whole of the debates. But if my brother and you
wish to go back again to the little journal, I should

not be discontented. I should lose some amusement, but I should save time and my eyes, for I
assure you, with that quantity of close printing, they
often ache before my '*séance du soir*' is over, for I
usually read them of an evening. There are some
very good speeches in the debate relative to emi-
grants. But I think I understand that these orators
read their speeches, at least those of any length.
Surely it would be far better if our orators did the
same. I agree with you that this whole business is
wonderful; and, I know not how it is, but success has
made me see this revolution in a somewhat different
light from what I saw it at first; I am more and more
convinced that Mr. Burke has gone a great deal too
far, especially in his abuse and contempt of the
National Assembly. Upon my word I think that were
our Parliamentary debates given at length in the same
way, they would cut but a shabby figure compared
with the Logographe—Mr Pitt and one or two more
excepted.

In your other opinion I cannot say that I agree
with you. I do not believe that any attempt at a
counter-revolution will be made; and I do believe, I
cannot help believing, that the king is now in earnest.
I cannot believe that any of the considerable European Powers will be foolish and romantic enough to
assist the princes, against their own interest in every
possible view; for I am convinced that if anything
would forward a revolution of the same kind in their

dominions, of which I fancy they have some dread, it would be this very step. As to the malcontents themselves, if they attempt anything by themselves, they must be mad indeed. What is an 'army of officers' without soldiers ? Should the king, indeed, head the party, this would be a different thing. But I do verily believe him to be in earnest ; if he is not I shall give him up as an arrant scoundrel, and hardly have any pity left for him. I don't say that I believe he in every respect approves of the change—that is another thing. No doubt, had he the power, he would restore the *noblesse* and the clergy. But I believe what he has said, that he is now convinced that a great majority of the people are determined in favour of the revolution, and that he has made up his mind to submit quietly to the change, and make the best of it for his own happiness and that of his family, and the peace and tranquillity of the kingdom. This is really not beyond my belief ; and whenever the event gives me the lie, I shall still think that I did right to be so choused. As to the king's venturing upon a second flight, it is the most incredible of all incredible things. He is no hero, and consider the hazard ! His death must be the inevitable consequence of detection. Your story about the grenadier is curious. What do you think those fellows would do if they had their majesties a second time in that situation ?

I have seen Mr. Cowper's 'Homer,' and little more.

Reymer lent me a copy for an hour or two. I compared a few places with Pope's version, but not enough to be any fair judge on the whole. The two translations are very different things, and on very different plans. Cowper is close, and must therefore be sometimes flat, and queer, and dry to an English reader. Pope is faithless, and must therefore read with more of the spirit of an original. A reader of Greek Homer, if he must read any version, would I suppose read Cowper's with most pleasure ; and a young student would certainly read it with most advantage, for Pope was no Grecian, and may often be caught translating from the Latin version. Yet the merit of his version has risen with me since this comparison. I suppose most English readers would prefer it much to Cowper's. But once more, I have seen so little, that I do not trust to my own judgment. There is a very sensible preface.

_____

FRAGMENT ON THE FRENCH REVOLUTION.

Colchester, February 17, 1792.

. . . Nowhere to be seen in Europe, but in wax-work, or upon the stage. But these are my fears, not my wishes, God knows. A man who likes levelling in society, *selon moi*, has as bad a taste as a man who likes a level country. For my part, I would not wish to live upon the surface of a wash-ball ; give me your ups and downs, moral and physical.

A JOURNEY IN A POSTCHAISE.

To his Brother.

Passenham, July 16, 1792.

Dear Brother,—It is high time you should know something about us and our locomotions. To-morrow morning, at six of the clock, we begin to *loco*-move towards Bitteswell. But this is not beginning first with the first in an Aristotelic manner. Take, in brief, our journal hither. Set out Monday, 9th, at six in the morning ; slept at Hockerill ; 10th, slept at Dunstable ; 11th, got hither in good time for dinner The weather was detestable and pestable , rain the whole way, except our first stage, and some part of one other. But we have the advantage of a most amply-protecting head, which, though there are no curtains, kept everything dry, save the hands and gloves of the driver. Our chaise performs well ; so do the horses—so does Mrs T All this is good ; and now, thank God, the weather is good, and Jupiter has withdrawn his urn, and is *sudus*, and hangs out his blue tapestry. We breakfast to-morrow at Northampton ; dine at Welford ; sleep at Bitteswell, where it would be a clever thing if Mr. R. T. could be of the party. But I must not hope for that. As to our stay, having another visit to pay, 100 miles farther, it cannot be above four or five days ; yet I think the good Pastor and his Pastorella will not be

content if we do not stay over a Sunday ; therefore,
if they are urgent, we shall not leave them till Monday, 23rd, when we positively set off for Emley ;
sleeping at Nottingham the first night, at Sheffield
the 2nd, and dining at Emley on the Wednesday.
Such is our plan. I thank you for the mention of a
cicerone at Nottingham. All the use I shall make
of your information is to take good heed to keep out
of the way of Mr. —— lest he should be obliging.
I suppose the lions of Nottingham are public, accessible lions, and require no interest to get a sight of.
You know my oddities pretty well. If there were
anything very curious, remarkably well worth seeing,
as a capital collection of pictures, &c., which could not
possibly be got at without Mr. ——'s help, I might
be glad to apply for it. As it is, I believe I shall not
disturb myself in what I always think one of the
greatest comforts of travelling, the being known to
nobody. Friends, indeed, and men that I like or
admire, *c'est autre chose.* And so I may still have
the effrontery to call upon Mr. Mason, though, in the
hurry of packing and preparing, I have unluckily
forgot to put up a little MS. paper of Mr. Gray's,
which was the pretence for my calling at Aston. I
forget whether I ever told you about this. Now I
have neither time nor space. But how nicely you
write difficult letters for one ! Bless me ! you shall
write all my letters ! I copied, verbatim almost, both
the epistles. Really, sir, I was ashamed of having

given you so much more trouble than I meant to give
you.   But it is certain that you saved me much time
and straining.   Thanks!   There was humour, me-
thought, in my copying two letters in that way.   I
chuckled as I wrote.   Alas! the poor Colchester
travellers!   You have heard of their distress; you
have heard also, I suppose, of their relief   They
must have been sadly plagued with rain, but are now
(wherever they are) looking about them comfortably.

Yours affectionately,

T. T.

A VISIT TO FRIENDS.—BITTESWELL AND NORTHAMPTON.

To his Brother.

Bitteswell, July 23, 1792.

Dear Brother,—Here we are still.   If it is a bad
thing to be detained, it is a good thing to be pleasantly
detained, or more properly to be detained where one
cannot but like to be.   Now here is very good well-
being at Bitteswell.   I was going to give you the
sequel of our history on Saturday, but I put it off for
the sake of having a past disaster to tell you of
rather than a present.   We were to have left this
place this very morning, but unfortunately, on Friday
night, our man was reported ill.   It seems he had
not been quite well since we left Passenham, though
he said nothing about it.   On Saturday a violent

eruption came out, which somewhat alarmed us on
Mary's account, lest it should be the measles, but the
man was quite sure that he had had them. I sent
for the Lutterworth Esculapius, who gave him what
was necessary, and declared that if this rash had not
found its way out the man would in all probability
have had a violent fever. He is now up and about,
and so well that we have no doubt of his being fit to
travel on Wednesday; he might be so to-morrow,
but we do not think it right to run the least risk, and
shall be guided by the doctor's opinion, who is to
call again by-and-by. So much for this disaster,
which I hope we may now consider as over and done
with. If you should write to Colchester soon, we
wish you to say only that we are quite well, and set
off for Yorkshire on Wednesday. That we were most
cordially received and are very happy here, I suppose
I need not tell you, nor that we like Mr. P.'s parsonage and garden, &c. I certainly shall not put you
to the hazard of jumping suddenly out of your chair
and respraining your ankle or your tendo Achillis,
or whatever it is, by telling you that I admire the
country round Bitteswell—the country immediately
round I ought to say; for by some perverse fate all
the ugliness seems confined to Mr. P.'s parish. This
I say from the experience of two very pleasant rides
I have had.

On Thursday we went in our two carriages
to Claybrook. I had a strong desire to see the

living place and the dying place of my poor friend
Jenner.[1] I was much gratified by the sight of his
house and church and monument, &c, though my
feelings had a tinge of melancholy, of course. The
village stands pleasantly, and forms a very pretty
and drawable object in some points of view, and the
country there is enclosed and clothed, and has none
of the baldness of its neighbouring parish.[2] Next day
Mr. P. took me a ride on horseback through green
lanes and villages and meadows, where we had peeps
of distant views, and in the villages the *merum rus*,
which I like. I tell Mr. P. that some gigantic evil
genius or demon must some time or other, out of spite
to the inhabitants of Bitteswell, on some account or
other, have risen in a passion one night or other and
have brushed away all the trees, plantations and
hedges with his great elbow. Now, you being a
poetical man, may work this up at your leisure into a
little poem called the 'Demon of Bitteswell,' whom
you may feign to have travelled hither as a travelling
tinker or pedlar from Northamptonshire, &c. Yesterday I preached here in the morning, and (after a
good peck) went with my landlord to Cotesbatch, and

[1] The Rev Charles Jenner, Incumbent of Claybrook, Leicester-
shire, an old college friend, and an amiable, accomplished man. A
tablet, with an inscription to his memory written by Lady Craven, is
in Claybrook Church.

[2] Bitteswell was then unenclosed, but an Enclosure Act followed
soon after Mr. Powell's presentation to the vicarage, and now there is
hardly a prettier country village and neighbourhood, of the unambitious
kind of scenery, to be seen anywhere.—R. T., 1881.

preached about idle words to Dr. Marriott, after a great treat on the harpsichord by Miss Greaterex, who was come thither, luckily, to teach. The good people were so civil as to press us to drink tea with them, so after dinner we all went and had a very pleasant afternoon, and I took my fiddle and accompanied (do you hear, Richard?) Miss G and the two Miss Marriotts, who play well, very well indeed. I assure you this was a treat to me, especially as it was quite unexpected. I like very well this specimen of Mr. P.'s neighbours. I have seen no others, but Mr. P. is gone to Rugby this morning to ask Dr. James for to-morrow. I had almost forgotten to tell you that Northampton likes me well. We breakfasted there and walked about 'Tis one of the neatest and handsomest towns I ever saw. We walked to the new hospital. I did not think the country about had been so pleasant and *riant*. The ride from Northampton to within a few miles of Welford is remarkably pleasant. But let me sketch our future plan. We are tempted to peep at Matlock ; this determines us for the Derby road, which is the better road, too, as Mr. P. tells us Thus, then Wed., b. Leicester d. Loughborough, s Derby ; Thurs., b where we can ; d. & s at Matlock; Frid, b. Dronfield, d. Bank Top, s. Emley. But should the weather be wet, we shall give up Matlock and proceed on the Thursday to Sheffield and get to Emley by dinner on Friday. So that our digression to Matlock will

M

make but half a day's difference in our stay at Elmsall's.

And now *addio.* Mary is studying a lesson in Metastasio, which I read with her. As you are no farmer (from which, by the way, you most illogically and impudently conclude that I am not), you will not ask me, I suppose, what appearances here are for harvest. I told Mr P. that there was an appearance of a very fine crop of posts and rails. 'Twill be well when they are once got in, and a few green hedges to be seen in their room. My chaise does well, my horses do well, above all Mrs. T. does well, and I hope John will do well, and then we shall all do well. To be continued (not after the M. R notion of continuation ; yet I should like that very well, for I should travel *sine die*) Loves from all to all

PART OF A LETTER DESCRIPTIVE OF A TOUR
IN AUGUST 1792.

Emley, August 2, 1792.

DEAR BROTHER,—Thursday the 29th was a day indeed! I have forgiven Jupiter Notus all his wrongs for the sake of that day, which seemed to have been made on purpose for us. The weather was cloudy, wild, windy, and unpleasant when we left Derby, and grew more so as we approached Matlock. We looked for nothing but disappointment, and expected to see nothing but from a window. But, in a most improb-

able and magic manner, just as we entered the Matlock Vale, out came the blessed luminary, away
scudded the clouds, piano ! cried the wind, and the
charming scene presented itself to us in all its beauty.
You know it, and so I am happily released from attempting description that describes nothing. Suffice
it to say that no two people could be more delighted
than we were. The whole day continued perfectly
fine and clear, and we made good use of our legs.
As soon as we had breakfasted, and made ourselves a
little trim, we sauntered till dinner. And, as soon as
we had dined, we boldly undertook to scale the
heights of Abraham. It was bold for Mrs. Twining
at least ; but, thank God, she was quite bonny, and
we actually performed the feat, and zigzagged up to
the very top, and nothing could answer better. I am a
stranger to mountains, and never yet seemed so bal-
looned and above the globe as in ascending this great
hill, for your mountaineers, I suppose, will allow it no
other name. If it is not sublime from its height, it is,
however, from its steepness, which almost made us
giddy.

We were at the first house, Saxton's—I mean
that which we came to first, for you know my maxim
of preferring secondary houses to first. Everybody
goes to Mason's ; now everybody is a body that I
never wish to meet. There was a moderate company
at Saxton's, where we had an excellent good *table
d'hôte* at dinner and supper. Indeed, it is a most com-

fortable house, and much better situated, I think, than Mason's. Upon the whole, no scheme ever answered better than this diversion to Matlock. I cannot pretend to tell you how intensely I (I may say we) enjoyed it, and how I feed my fancy, and shall do as long as my memory lasts, with the recollection of it.

The next day, Friday, was quite another sort of day; not that the weather was very bad, though showery and troublesome, but we had forty-five miles to go ; the road all very hilly, and the greatest part of it very bad. Baited at a village called Dronfield, at a little alehouse fifteen miles and a half from Matlock. Dined at Bank Top (eighteen miles) about six o'clock. Thence we had twelve miles to Emley. We found the road very bad ; night overtook us, and after much distress, perpetual enquiries, and dread of being wrecked, we arrived here at eleven o'clock, and found everybody snoring. After much hallooing and knocking and noise, however, we got admission ; and after eating a crust of bread, &c., went very happy to bed, and rose still more happy in the morning. How silly it was of me to forget the sort of roads we had to go through. Elmsall said he knew, as soon as he heard of our intention of making one day from Matlock hither, that we should be taken in, but he had no means of setting us right. Well, all is well that ends well ; and here we are, as well and as happy as we can be. R Hey is with us. We have good conversation and good music, but have not yet sufficiently recovered from the soreness of our last day's journey to think of getting again into our chaise. We have been prevailed upon to stay a week longer than we purposed, and I have written to Colchester to provide for my church another Sunday, viz. the 19th. So we shall leave Emley on Monday, August 20, or Tuesday the 21st, and get to Colchester on Friday the 24th. There, now you know how and where to have me. And so, adieu! I hope you have done something that will do something for your lameness. Mr. Jarvis Cox Jervas, the Lutterworth apothecary, recommended tight lacing. Mr. Elmsall desires his compliments, and Mrs. Twining her love, with mine, to all. I hope to find my mother at Colchester.— Yours affectionately,

T. T.

Oh, poor France! and poor King of France! what shall we say to them now!

THE POSTCHAISE TOUR CONCLUDED.—THE FRENCH REVOLUTION.—DESPOTISM AND LIBERTY.

To his Brother.

Colchester, Aug. 30, 1792.

Dear Brother,—This gap in my continuation is a little *Monthly Review*-ish. But before I got home I seemed to have little or nothing to tell you ; and since I got home I have been partly busy, and partly in an idle unsettled kind of way, such as travelling always leaves me in. Even now it requires the utmost exertion of all the nerves and muscles of my mind to bring me to the resolution of sitting down to write a letter. It will, I am afraid, be yet some time before I perfectly recover myself, so as to relish my common pursuits and *train de vie.* But let me continue my journal, though a mere journal. I need not tell you that I stayed at Emley a week longer than I purposed. We left that place on Monday se'nnight, the 20th. My Mr Elmsall has a brother who lives at Briorley, a village fourteen miles from Emley and ten from Doncaster. There we dined, but rather too late, on account of the badness of the road from Emley. The house is perched upon a high hill, and commands a vast basin, full of prospect. 'Twas beautiful, but our old luck attended us It rained incessantly the whole day, after three weeks of fine weather, which ended precisely when we left Emley. Mr. Elmsall was so kind as to send his servant with us almost to Doncaster, and well it was that he did, for the latter part of the way, over (I think) Pigbarn heath or common, was so unmarked and turfy that I must have trusted to chance for my way, and should probably have been benighted a second time The road, however, was all very good, and we got well to Doncaster before dark, after a ride that would have been delightful if the rain had permitted us to look about us

Oh ! what a torment it is, in a country both beautiful and new, to be stooping and poking till one's back aches, only to see that one can't see! Tuesday, b. Barnby Moor (the most comfortable and private public house, take it altogether, that I ever was at), d. Scarthing Moor, s. Newark ; the weather mended, the afternoon and evening fine, the ride to Newark as pleasant as possible, the road admirable ; Wed , b Grantham, d Witham Common (a very good new inn), s. Stamford, (good weather) ; Thurs., b. Stilton, d. Huntingdon, s. Cambridge, and next day, in short, we got home about 7 o'clock—a long pull (48 miles), but we did it easily by setting out very early, and going to Haverill (20 miles) to breakfast. And—*sic transit gloria mundi*—in spite of the perverseness of the weather, our tour was on the whole very pleasant to us. Our object was more to see persons than places, yet we have seen many places we never saw before, and had great pleasure in seeing again some which we had seen I am afraid you will abuse me, however, when I tell you that we did not make the use we might have made of the fine weather we had at Emley.

We only went one day to Wakefield ; I did fully intend to have seen Ealand again, but somehow I let it slip. Elmsall has had a terrible rheumatic complaint, and seemed not inclined to stir. Then we found the roads about Emley so bad as to discourage us, and we were very happy at home. Richd. Hey was with us the whole time. He was very busy every morning in writing a pamphlet against Paine and the

'Rights of Man.' What I read I thought excellent, and I hope he will finish and publish. By the way, I have got his two printed dialogues, or dramacles, for you I should certainly not have remained so quietly at Emley if I had not seen Matlock. That satisfied my seeing appetite so fully that nothing seemed worth looking at after it. I had, however, great pleasure from walks about Emley ; the lakes were not attainable, and I could see nothing in the neighbourhood of Emley that I had not seen before. Pray observe one thing as to our rash stretch from Matlock to Emley *eodem die,* that it was entirely Mr. P.'s doing. Our plan was this : b. Chesterfield, d. Sheffield, s Bank Top ; but Mr. P laughed at us, and said it was pity to sleep within 12 miles of Emley, and that we might easily do it, &c. But I was sorry I listened to him, for his notions about long stages, &c, do not suit mine. He never considered the hillyness and roughness of the roads, &c. If I have any wish about my chaise it is that it was somewhat less high. My horses seem much the better for the business they have done. Mrs. T , too, is jollified and wholesomely embrowned by her travels ; but no sooner did she get home than a sore throat and considerable degree of fever made her quite ill for a day or two ; that complaint is nearly over, and now she is sitting with her leg upon a press, and dare not stir about, which to her is no small punishment. At an inn just before we got home she stumbled over the black chaise trunk and hurt her leg a little. It grew worse and worse, and is now so inflamed and swelled that Mr Newell says she must make as little use of it as possible. This is a great grievance to us. But now we talk of legs, what have you to say of yours? I am really very uneasy about you. My mother says you do not mend at all. I desire to know whether you have or have not tried other advice. If you have not I shall scold. I am seriously apprehensive that the so long non-use of your leg may be attended with some lasting ill-effect of weakness or lameness. Pray stir your stumps and do something efficacious.

Well, but France, what say you now? For my part, whether I can justify my politics or not, I am really obliged to wish, and with all my heart, that the Austrians and Prussians may carry everything before them, get into Paris, set free the unhappy King and Queen, and chastise the ferocious and butcherly mob, and take the whole club of Jacobins prisoners at once. I really wished the French well, even the reforming French, while their views were moderate; but this despotism of his majesty the people —I cannot endure it. It puts me all in a ferment when I hear or read of it. If you can cool me, do. Elmsall and R. Hey and I were in perfect unison. Elmsall says there never can be any peace or quiet in the world till the word liberty is entirely abolished and expunged from all languages. I do really think that no word ever did mankind so much harm. Pray

let me have the precious packet from Mr. Hughes.
Consider, sir! The Emley people think me the foinest
man that e'er coom'd into a pulpit. Let me hear
from you soon.

PALEY'S TRACT.—PROSPECTS OF WAR

To the Rev. Mr. Hughes.

Colchester, Feb. 10, 1793.

Dear Sir,—I see Archdeacon Paley is come forth
with a little twopenny thing *ad populum*, called
' Reasons for Contentment,' which I sent for the
moment I saw it advertised.   He is, in *my* scale of
men, a capital man ; and I am glad he has con-
descended to take up his pen in that way.   This
war, which, I suppose, is now inevitable, hangs heavy
upon my mind.   I own, I cannot see that there *is*, or
rather that there was, a *necessity* for it ; and nothing
short of necessity, I think, can justify war.   If I am
mistaken in that, I wish all mankind were mistaken
with me.   I met with a passage lately in old Isocrates,
that pleased me much ; perhaps, because it *surprised*
me ; for such sentiments were not very common in
those times of valour and hard-heartedness.   As I
know you would not thank me for bothering you with
Greek, I have taken it into my head to translate it
for you ; and here it is.   If it is good for anything,
it must be good in English.   But I had not time to
be nice about it.

' Numerous as are the evils to which human nature is necessarily exposed, we have invented many *unnecessary* evils in addition to them,—the evils of war, civil dissension, and sedition. Hence, we see some massacred by lawless violence at *home* ; others, exiled and wandering with their wives and children in a *foreign* land ; many, reduced by want to the necessity of fighting for wages, and laying down their lives in defence of their *enemies* against their *friends*. Yet, for all these things, we feel no concern, we express no indignation. Our tears are always ready for the imaginary calamities, which the fictions of the poets set before us ; while the thousand real and dreadful distresses of war, of which we are eye-witnesses, are so far from exciting our compassion, that we even receive more pleasure from the misery we bring upon others, than for the happiness we enjoy ourselves.'

Good-night. Let me hear from you soon. Compliments to Mrs. H.

THE FATE OF LOUIS XVI —ENGLAND AND FRANCE. —RUMOURS OF WAR.

To his Brother.

February 12, 1793.

Great and strange things have happened since I wrote to you last! I know how you felt for that poor murdered king , for my·part I was affected by it in a very odd way : I could hardly bring myself to

talk about it or write about it. One may be reduced
to silence by having too much as well as too little to
say. And how those villains glory in that deed of
complicated injustice, cruelty, and folly ! Do you see
how Brissot talks ? the avowed correspondent of — —.
The Tower opens its gates wide for some of these corresponding lords and gentlemen. But alas ! this war
—this war—I cannot reconcile myself to it, I cannot
see the necessity of it ; it may now be necessary, but
I am afraid that necessity was unnecessarily brought
on. It is terrible to think that we should be plunged
into war by etiquette, and the *qui vive*, and the honour
and dignity of the nation ; yet I am really afraid that
this is the truth. It is terrible to have reason (and
there seems to be reason) to think that we might have
avoided this calamity, for calamity it is at any rate,
by a little less of the thing called spirit, and a little
more of the thing called prudence. I have no idea of
being provoked into a war, of going to war because
we are angry. I think I am without prejudice, Minis-
terial or anti-Ministerial ; if I have any prejudice, it
is certainly on the former side ; and I now have so
high an opinion of Mr. Pitt, that I am ready to suspect he has better reasons on his side than I am
aware of. But I dread the consequence of this war,
which will be a war with desperate men, who have
fought, and will fight, desperately. ' Una salus victis
nullam sperare salutem.' War will unite the French
nation, and what is the object ? to check and humble

them and their mad principles? It may, but it may not; nay, if it does not, I tremble to think what may follow.

I tremble to think what effect ill-success may produce upon ourselves. In short, it does appear to me that there is much sense and truth in what Mr. Fox has said upon this subject. I have not read his letter, but I will read it. As to war, I hold that nothing can justify it but absolute necessity; is there, or rather was there, that necessity? I am really, as you may perceive, distressed by my anxiety and fears upon this subject. If you think differently, for God's sake try to make me think differently. But I rather suspect that we are something congenial in our feelings. Mr. Hughes, I find, is of the doubting and fearing party. (See a fine passage, I think, which I sent him from old Isocrates.)

ENGLAND AND FRANCE —BISHOP HORSLEY'S
SERMONS.—PALEY ON CONTENTMENT.

Colchester, February 19, 1793.

DEAR BROTHER,—How provoking that, after being silent so long, we should both open our mouths at the same moment. I am always angry at this crossing of letters. I was very glad, however, at any rate, to see your pen again. Your politics were almost an answer to my politics. Yet the answer does not entirely satisfy me. I hope the war was necessary and inevitable, but I rather trust it is so, than see it is so. With your 'if' (if they, the Ministry, clearly foresaw, &c., &c.) it will do. But I still find myself backward to believe that the French had any ambitious designs upon us, any design to attack us, as the Ministry seem to think they had ; or rather, perhaps, I should say, that they would have entertained any such designs, if we had kept upon good terms with them. 'But how, as they have conducted themselves, was it possible to keep upon such terms with them?' I know not how to answer my own question. I will believe, as you do, that our rulers know more than we know. But then I ask myself again, and am at a loss for an answer, 'If they do know more than has yet appeared, is it not natural to suppose that they would produce these stronger reasons for their own justification?' If they know more, one does not see why they should not say more.

I am always sorry to see the word dignity used in speaking of the necessity of war. I cannot allow the dignity of the nation to have anything to do with the matter. I cannot allow anything but the necessity of self-defence to be a justifiable cause of war. The defence of allies comes to much the same thing. Well, *jacta est alea*, and God speed us. We have nothing now to wish but that these butchers and savages may be completely checked and humbled with all speed, so as to produce a safe and lasting peace.

The discourse arrived safe ; I have not yet made

any use of it. Mr. H 's addition is good, though some of it I must alter a little. Have you read the Bishop of St. David's [1] sermons ? He is a strong and muscular writer, but with too little candour and moderation, too much dogmaticality, too overbearing a manner, to please me thoroughly. He is sometimes really eloquent. There is a fine stroke about the Queen of France, I mean this sentence at the conclusion of his French scene : ' The royal widow's anguish embittered by the rigours of a close imprisonment ; with hope, indeed, at no great distance of release —of such release as has been given to her lord ' I do think that very fine. His doctrine goes too near to passive obedience for me ; nay, for truth, for reason, and for the times. Paley talks more rationally upon this subject. Have you read Paley's ' Reasons for Contentment ? ' If not, lose no time ; you will be charmed, for I was. I wonder whether that is good logic. I was even moved by some parts of it. Nothing brings the tears into my eyes sooner than that sort of writing upon that sort of subject.

A LETTER OF CONDOLENCE ON A SISTER'S DEATH.

To his Nephew, Thomas Twining, in India.

Colchester, May 20, 1793

Your father thinks I shall be in time to write a few lines to you, and, indeed, a few only they can be ;

[1] Bishop Horsley.

but there are times and occasions when even a few words may say enough to give us some comfort, if only as a testimony of regard and affection from those whose regard and affection we in any degree wish for and value. I grieve that you, who have so well deserved to receive nothing but good news from home, should now have received tidings which I know must affect you much,[1] not only on your own account, but still more on account of those who of course suffer more and feel more from the loss than yourself. I have not, nor ever had, much opinion of what is called consolation upon such occasions; consolation in words and advice and wise sayings about grief, &c. Such feelings will have, and ought to have, their way. If they are so easily talked away, they are not deeply felt, and might safely have been left to themselves. Another sort of consolation I have no opinion of— the consolation of trying to forget a loss of this sort ; the pitiful comfort of avoiding as much as possible the recollection and the mention of persons dear to us, and who ought to be dear to our memory. There is nothing wrong in such situations, or that fairly gives occasion for dissuasive advice or remonstrance, except (what is not uncommon) the indulgence of grief beyond what is necessary ; that is, beyond what the mind, if left to itself, and to that providential disposition which inclines us naturally to relieve ourselves and admit comfort when it offers itself, would feel.

---

[1] The death of his sister Emma, from fever.

Unfortunately this is the case only with people who feel a great deal, and therefore have no need to have their pain aggravated and prolonged by a false notion of the duty of struggling against comfort, and feeding grief by voluntary brooding over melancholy ideas.

THE DELIGHTS OF BEAUTIFUL SCENERY IN THE ABSENCE OF CROWDS.—FRENCH ANARCHY.

To his Brother.

Colchester, June 7, 1793.

Dear Brother,—I hope this letter will have to travel on to Maidenhead, because I am sure the longer stay you make there the better for you all. I thank you for your letter ; short as it was, it gave me much pleasure. You need not have apologised for its shortness. I would have you better employed there than in sitting down to write long letters. If your letter had been only this :—

Maidenhead Bridge,
May 27, 1793.

Dear Brother,

I am, dear brother, &c.,
R. T.

it would have been a good letter to me, for I was anxious to hear that you had turned your backs upon melancholy scenes, and knew that you could not have been in any spot not far from home that would be more likely to do you the good and give you just the

N

sort of pleasure that you wanted. What is commonly called amusement, gay, public, bustling amusement, was not what you wanted, nor even what you could have endured. I know of no amusement so adapted to soothe and tranquillise the mind, to restore it gradually to its state of usual cheerfulness, as that which you have been now enjoying. I have always said that the pleasure I receive (and I believe you to be in the same case) from beautiful scenes of nature, viewed in quiet and retirement (for surround me with good company, and a crowd of ladies and gentlemen, and Matlock itself becomes worse than Hockley in the Hole)—I have always said that this pleasure is something totally *sui generis* to me, something which I can neither analyse nor describe nor account for. The general effect I feel from it at the time is a serenity, a perfect complacency, a full satisfaction that wants nothing, looks forward to nothing, leaves no wish to be anything or anywhere but what I am and where I am then ; all this mixed with more benevolence than I can feel perhaps in any other situation. Set me in a romantic valley, I could pluck out my eyes and give them to my friend if I could see the prospect without them. Another ingredient is a sort of religious feeling. Men may be atheists possibly in their closets, but an atheist upon Abraham's Heights at Matlock, or in the Vale of Ealand, I cannot conceive. Temples and churches are poor contrivances. Let me preach and pray in the open air of heaven, with

woods and rocks and waterfalls around me, upon the
holy ground that God has consecrated.

> These are Thy glorious works, Parent of good,
> Almighty—thine this universal frame,
> Thus wondrous fair ! Thyself how wondrous then ?

I beg your pardon for this rhapsody. Take it as a
demonstration of what I said, that I could not describe
what I feel. *Quod erat demonstrandum*, as the mathe-
maticians say. I rejoice to hear a good account
of you all from my mother. Stay where you are as
long as you can I preached for the poor French
priests here, and got them about 20 guineas—more
than I expected in so small a parish, and the best
collection in Colchester—owing, to be sure, chiefly to
my eloquence. You must allow that my sermon
closed with a quotation pat to French anarchy.
' Lastly, let us in the true spirit of Christianity recommend, not ourselves only, but even our enemies also,
to the merciful protection of that Almighty Being
who judgeth among the nations ; who alone can hide
us from the gathering together of the froward and
from the insurrection of wicked doers ; who stilleth
the raging of the sea, and what is still more calami-
tous in its effects, and almost as much beyond human
power to set bounds to, " the madness of the people.

BOSWELL S 'LIFE OF JOHNSON.'—PINDAR.

To his Brother.

October 16, 1793.

. . . I read, however, and am now *tandem aliquando* reading, Boswell's 'Life of Johnson ;' which, having shrunk into octavo, I have bought, for you know I hate all books that are too big to hold in my hand. Have you read it ? I am prodigiously entertained and gratified. I laugh, it is true, at Boswell sometimes. He must be a singular character. Sometimes he says very silly things, and asks silly questions, and carries admiration and wonder to a ridiculous excess. He could never take ' Nil admirari ' for his motto. Yet there is a *naïveté*, a candour, and a *bonhomie* in the man that makes me like him ; and all that relates to Dr. Johnson, between his singularities, and his admirable sense, and undulness of conversation, is highly amusing to me. I have met with those who call this book tiresome : I never read a book that was less so. Johnson's readiness of argument and repartee in conversation is surprising.

For about an hour after my breakfast, which is generally over by eight o'clock, it is a sort of general rule with me to read some Greek author, and my present author is Pindar (not Peter), of whom I never read much in my former days. There are here and there fine poetical strokes in him, and moral maxims well expressed ; but he is very unequal, often very tiresome, very obscure, and to us moderns very uninteresting. On the whole, he is marked in my list as one of those ancient authors whose real merit falls short of their echoed character. He is sometimes bombastic, and sometimes prosaic. But perhaps I am telling you what you care nothing about.

I must give you a passage from a letter I received from E. this morning. He is at Buxton, for a rheumatic complaint. The other day, much against his will, he was taken in to read prayers in the public rooms. ' So,' says he, ' I was forced to stick myself up behind a little desk, only like a table, with my legs exposed, to read prayers (for I took care not to bring any sermons with me) to 150 gentlemen and ladies, in a fine large assembly room, with handsome sofas, chandeliers, &c. It is a fine thing in a church to have everything covered but one's head. It felt quite indecent to be so much exposed.'

THE STATE OF POLITICS IN EUROPE IN 1793

To Dr. Burney.

Colchester, October 30, 1793.

My time has not been particularly taken up, so that I have no excuse there. Where, then ? Why, in short, I have no excuse but inexcusable indolence and dilatoriness. Yet an indolent man, in general, I am not. But I have, and have always had, a backwardness, which I cannot account for, to sit down and begin to write a letter of any length. I wish one could find some way of doing things without beginning to do them. I could do anything so, at any time. But stop! let me not fill my whole paper with this foolery.

.   .   .   .   .   .

But alas! the wretched state of this European world of ours engrosses one's whole attention. I dread the meeting of Parliament—I dread war—I dread peace—I dread everything. The world cannot stand against these specious but false theories of government, that have got possession of men's minds everywhere. I have long been of opinion that Locke, in his famous treatise, sowed the first seeds of this madness. Admitting (what I cannot admit) that such notions of government are true in themselves, yet they are truths for which the world is not yet ready—I mean that the world is not yet wise enough, good enough, moderate enough to make it safe that such notions should be entrusted to them. I am ready to gnaw my flesh when I think that all the power of Europe cannot crush the cannibals that at present govern France. What think you of their horrid charge against the poor Queen? Her real character I do not know, nor can we say what is, or is not, possible to the corruption of human nature , but will any man in his senses believe this story upon the faith of the unprincipled and murderous villains from whom we have it? It is too shocking to talk of.

And what are you about? Surely you have not dropped Metastasio? I shall be sorry if you have; it would have been a pleasant book. We had need do all we can to amuse ourselves and one another, in these sour and ill-blooded times, when throat-cutting seems to be that great old baby, Master Man's, chief amusement. Addio. Remember me and Mrs. T. to all, and do let us be a little acquainted, and 'do as shall become those that would do reason ; and I hope, upon familiarity, will grow more contempt.'—I am ever yours most sincerely,

T. T.

A FRIEND'S TRAGEDY.—A VISIT TO CAMBRIDGE.

To his Brother.

Colchester, Dec. 20, 1793.

Dear Brother,—Imprimis—Take notice that I have sent by to-day's coach a parcel directed outwardly to you and inwardly to R. Hey at York. It containeth his tragedy and my remarks and criticisms thereon, and a letter therewith, and I entreat you to forward it forthwith to a York coach, as I have detained the precious MS. longer than I intended, and I know he will be upon thorns till he receives it. You will be so good as to let no time be lost. I think it is sufficiently packed, but if, on removing the envelope directed to you, you should think it would be better guarded with an additional brown coat, you will be so good as to order one ; but I daresay there is no occasion. As you said you 'hoped you should see more of it,' I should have had no scruple in sending the parcel unsealed that you might have read or looked at the MS, but your time is too much taken up, and R. H. will be impatient, so that it must set off for York as soon as possible. R. H said that if I had no objection to alter little faults to my mind (supposing no material alteration to be wanting), and if I could find access to a manager, he had for his part no objection to my conveying the MS immediately to such manager But he left me at full liberty, and I told him that even had I found an *aditus* to a manager, I could not have taken such a terrible responsibility upon my shoulders. I could only submit my free remarks to him, and leave him to judge and alter for himself.

He wrote this tragedy while on a visit to Mr. Mason, who read it and found much fault, upon which he corrected and altered a good deal. He has told me Mr. M——'s objections, but I would not read them till I had finished my own critique. On the whole the thing, I think, has great merit, but not a common sort of merit, and therefore not calculated to be popular. This is the character, perhaps, of all he writes. He puts me often in mind of Shakspere—no small praise. He is like him at times in expression, in fancy, and in natural strokes. Have you read 'Democratic Rage'? I took it in my pocket to Cambridge, and read three acts upon the road, but was so careless as to leave it behind me at Dr. H——'s rooms. It has neither the faults nor the beauties of R. H——'s; a far inferior and less original thing to me; but I suppose Messieurs the public would like it better. 'An audience,' as I told R. H——, 'like to look straight at a thing; not to be kept squinting between a true story and a false story by a story that is neither.'

But enough of this. The history of my Cambridge expedition is this : I was once in company with a lady who was asked to 'favour us with a song.' The word 'song' had scarcely got clear of the lips of the asker when the lady answered by beginning to sing, 'Water parted from the sea.' It made us all jump, like a gun that should go off if one only touched the trigger. We snapped our eyes, cock'd our ears, smiled and listened. So, upon Dr. Hey's saying in a letter to me, 'Could not you come and stay a little time with us ?' I immediately wrote him word that I would come and stay a week with him. Accordingly, sir, on Monday, Dec. 2nd, I set out *solus* in my chaise, with shirts, &c. and my fiddle, and drank tea with the Doctor in good time the next day. I stayed at Cambridge till Wednesday the 11th, and got safe and well home the next day by dinner, after as pleasant and as completely answering a scheme as I ever enjoyed in my life. The weather was excellent, the roads good; my horse performed well. I caught no cold; met with no rubs or *désagrémens* of any kind. I passed my time most pleasantly in Cambridge, where

I think I had not made so long a stay since I ceased to reside there. I enjoyed my friend's *tête-à-tête* and music of the best kind almost every evening, public concerts and private quartett parties. In the morning I walked about viewing improvements, lounging in book-shops and music-shops, and with singular delight brushed up reminiscences of old walks and places and things. Everybody was very kind and civil to me. I dined with the Master of Sidney, who was very hospitable and pleasant, and seemed glad to see me. I supped with my old friend Professor Mainwaring and his young lady. I never saw him look so well in my life. I believe I did tell you that the sale of my book is reviving at Cambridge.

Not the worst part of my entertainment was my attendance upon two of Dr. Hey's Norrisian lectures in Sidney College Hall. Nothing could to me be more opposite to everything that is dull, heavy, tiresome, trite, &c. He has no papers, no notes at all. He looks over his written lectures before he goes into the hall, but all is perfectly easy, clear, unembarrassed. His manner exactly the thing, with just enough of authority, without anything pompous or dogmatical. His audience were very attentive, and most of them took notes. The Professor stands at a small desk, and has a bench near him, on which are placed such books, Latin, English or Greek, as he has occasion to quote; and in the course of his lecture he takes them up and reads the passages. This relieves and makes a very pleasant variety. The lectures were extremely entertaining to me. He mixes extempore talk with his memoriter, and alters *sur le champ* the language of his written lectures ; but all seemed very well of a piece ; there was no jolt in passing from written to unwritten. I assure you I was very much pleased, and could not help expressing my surprise that he had not a larger audience. They were mostly young men, and many came scattering in the midst of the lecture, for which I told him I should *job* them. I told Hey what I said to you of ——, and, candid man as he is, he would not say that I had overcharged the picture. *I nunc,* &c., I have emptied my budget at last. Remember us to mother and to all. I hope my mother is safe and well in town. I long for better news from Bitteswell. Write.

A LETTER OF GOOD COUNSEL.

To his Nephew, Daniel Twining.[1]

Colchester, November 4, 1795.

. . . There is a great deal in setting off well ; not merely because it makes a young man respected by others, but still more because it makes him respect himself; it gives him the best and most useful of all sorts of pride—that of keeping up good character

----

[1] He went from Rugby with an Exhibition to Pembroke Coll. Cambridge, of which he was afterwards a Fellow.

acquired, and of exerting himself to go on and acquire more.

It is very certain that a young man, at his first enlargement from the restraints of a school, to the (I had almost said) no restraints of a University life, is exposed to considerable dangers, from which nothing can secure him but a good disposition, assisted by a great deal of resolute prudence. It neither should nor can be concealed from you (for you must soon see it is so) that if any young person is disposed to abuse the liberty of a college life, there is hardly any kind of vice or folly that he has it not in his power to practise, if he chooses it. It is a wide and common field ; the gates all wide open, and the fences (now I fear) almost all thrown down, and even while some of them remained standing they were easily climbed over. A man must have the *murus aëneus* in his own breast ; and so (for you will think I am preaching) as much brass in your inside, and as little in your face, my dear, as you please. I think in college it used to be the fashion in my time to wear it chiefly upon the face. I always recollect with some pleasure that upon my first going to college I was fortunate enough to fall into a valuable set of acquaintance, the friendship of some of whom (Dr. Hey, for example) has been a great happiness to me all my life ; and that I was very shy of others whom I knew not, or knew no good of, and kept them aloof as much as possible. With whom a man will be acquainted is not always in his choice ;

but with whom he will be intimate always is. But enough of this. Now let me say that though my advice as to conduct may be thrown away upon you (or thrown away as a bushel of coals sent to Newcastle would be), my literary advice may possibly be of some use to you. Therefore, if in the course of your studies (your classical studies I mean chiefly) you should meet with difficulties, as to the sense of particular passages or words or phrases, where commentators and lexicons may not satisfy you ; or in writing Latin, or as to choice of books, &c., I shall always be pleased to hear from you, and have a particular pleasure in giving you any assistance in my power. It is an opportunity that I often wanted and wished for when I was a young student, but never had. I was obliged to fight my way through thick and thin, *proprio marte*, the only sort of Mars that a Twining is constructed to have anything to do with. I have sent your father some few remarks upon your verses. If any of them do not satisfy you, or if I am hypercritical, tell me so fairly, and defend yourself manfully. I was never one of your positive critics.

Yours, dear D, affectionately,

T. T.

POLITICS IN ENGLAND.—'THE TWO BILLS.'

From Richard Twining.

November 27, 1795.

The meeting in Palace Yard[1]. . . . Could Mr Fox
and the Duke of Bedford possibly imagine that, from
such a meeting, the sense of the inhabitants of Westminster was to be collected? Mr Wilkes was once
told by his adversaries that they would 'take the
sense of the ward.' 'Do,' replied Wilkes, 'and I will
take the *nonsense* of the ward, and beat you ten to
one!' This subject leads me naturally enough to
my twelfth head, the times. I am most sorry to see
such times; but if I were to indulge myself in expressing my sorrow, if I were to say all I think, my
letter (pretty long already) would swell beyond—far
beyond—letter size; and yet I cannot remain wholly
silent. To be as brief, then, as I can, I think I may
make a new division of the inhabitants of this island:
I may divide them into the supporters and the opposers of the two Bills now before Parliament. I
consider the supporters of the Bills as persons wishing
to preserve the constitution of this country, and to

---

[1] See *Annual Register*, Nov. 15, 1795. A meeting of the electors
of Westminster, attended by the Duke of Bedford, Mr. Fox, Mr. Grey,
and Mr. Sheridan, to protest against the two Bills then pending in the
House for the better security of His Majesty's person and the suppres-
sion of seditious assemblies. They were known as the 'Treason' and
'Sedition' Bills, both rigorous enactments, strenuously opposed by Mr.
Fox, but carried into operation without exciting any strong feeling in
the country.

secure us from that scene of horror which must attend its overthrow. I consider the opposers of the Bills either as persons intending and anxiously wishing to promote general confusion, or as persons willing to risk even such confusion in order to get into place. Though I think I am right as to my general description of the opposers of the Bills, yet I am willing to admit that there are amongst them many who do not deliberately mean to do what is wrong, but who are completely deluded. The conduct of these people should be added to the crimes of those who delude them. Is it possible that any person wishing to live in peace, and wishing to preserve the constitution of his country, can think that the meetings which have been held for some time past should still be held, and that the opinions which have been spread so industriously should continue to be spread ? Now it is evident that the laws already in force, interpreted by juries as we find they are, are insufficient to prevent these meetings, and to stop the open communication of these opinions. According to my notion, any Constitution that would not admit, upon any account whatever, of any alteration, would be a bad Constitution ; it would be a bad Constitution for such beings as men. I have adopted the present and popular meaning of a Constitution—a thing made up, one would think, of a given unalterable quantity of rights, privileges, liberties, &c. ; whereas the Constitution is rather, as I imagine, composed of King, Lords, and

Commons, who have a right to alter the quantities of rights and liberties. When certain rights, and privileges, and liberties were secured to us by our ancestors (whether by charters, or the Bill of Rights, or in any other way, it matters not), the object was that we should be the better, *i e.* the happier, for them. If those ancestors could have foreseen that their descendants would, at some distant day, use a part of those rights and liberties to confound all right and all liberty, that the best part of the Constitution would be employed to overthrow the Constitution itself, and that thus, what was intended to form would actually destroy our happiness—if our venerable ancestors could have foreseen all this, would they have secured to us so many rights and so much liberty? Certainly not. But, unfortunately, we see what they could not foresee. These things strike me so forcibly that unless the present Bills pass without their being so modified and weakened as to render them ineffectual, I consider that the adversary must prevail God only knows— for I am very serious when I think of these matters—how they will end ! Opinions which, if the sneak Law does not call them so, sober reason must call seditious, are preached publicly every night; and they are devoured with avidity. At this very moment I firmly believe that nothing but the military keeps us quiet ; there is a vast force in and near town Well ; but if the Bills do pass—what then ? There, again, the prospect is uncomfortable ; for even in

Parliament the doctrine of resistance has been preached, and much industry and ingenuity have been exerted to prevent the Bills from answering the end intended, if they should pass. I hope, however, that Mr. Pitt will be firm and successful. That way we have some chance ; the other, we have none at all.

DEMOSTHENES AND CICERO.

To his Nephew Daniel Twining, at Cambridge.

Colchester, Dec. 12, 1795

. . . Thank you for Dr. P.'s speech. ' Chaos ' is well applied to the confusion and perverseness of obscurity of the style of Thucydides, but ' beauty ' does not seem exactly the word to be applied to *Demosthenes* (if it *was* to *him*, for you express some doubt). I admire Demosthenes—I should call him a *fine* writer, eloquent, nervous, vehement, δεινός, &c. But *beauty* implies something more smooth, finished, polished and rhetorical, &c. Demosthenes was a rough dashing fellow, very different from Cicero. There is no *appearance* of art in Demosthenes : in Cicero a great deal too much. (I speak now of Cicero's *orations* chiefly.)

O

ON RECEIVING AND ANSWERING LETTERS.

To his Brother.

Colchester, October 1, 1797.

I received your letter of answerings this morning, and I thank you for it. I think R. H.'s (and Dr. H.'s) notion of correspondence a very good one, and, in general, I believe I keep pretty exactly to the rule myself. If any one thing be essential to what we call corresponding, it is this of answering everything in one's correspondent's letter that requires answering. A correspondence is only a written conversation. Now, in conversation it is thought rude if you remain silent when a question is asked. But I go further than this. I say that a man should be answered, even when he asks nothing. In conversation, if a man makes a remark, expresses an opinion, a sentiment, a notion, he expects something— approbation or disapprobation, assent or dissent—from the person to whom he is talking. ' Pray do you go to town to-morrow?' Mum.—' I am afraid it will rain to-day' Mum —' I think this is the finest country I ever saw.' Mum.— This is but a flat sort of conversation In writing, the case is worse, because what a man writes is generally better sort of stuff, and better worth answering or noticing It has often struck me that correspondents have not a proper notion of this matter in general. Often they do not take any notice at all even of questions directly put. That is inexcusable, though I excuse every man who serves me so. Yet it frets me a little at the time. But no doubt I am sometimes guilty of the same thing myself. But nothing is more common than to pass over unnoticed everything that has not a ? at the end of it, though it be very plain that, in fact, a question is implied in it, viz. the question, ' Don't you think so ? ' or ' Do you differ from me ? ' Well, I have made a very fine bit of dissertation, not a syllable of which I had the least intention to make.

A HOLIDAY TOUR IN ENGLAND AND WALES.

From a Diary kept in 1797.

A curious circumstance at our inn (the Star and Garter, Worcester) diverted us. Here are no he-waiters—a great recommendation ; and all the maids wear an ornamental sort of appendage to their caps, a long piece of muslin, or something, which is not fastened close under the chin, but hangs down very low—a kind of muslin chain. When they are busy they throw it back over their heads, to be out of their way. We thought it singular, and did not observe it to be a general fashion in the place. Upon interrogating one of the damsels that waited upon us, she told us that it was peculiar, and had been so for many years, to the servants at that particular inn, and that it was not worn anywhere else. A more pleasant

piece of traditional distinction I never met with.
But—

> Mos unde deductus per omne
> Tempus . . .
>   . . . quærere di tuli ;
> Nec scire fas est omnia.—HOR. IV. Ode 4.

.   .   .   .   .

We proceeded to Shrewsbury, where we dined,
and stayed till next day. This was a capital ride,
along the beautiful vale of the Severn, the river all
the way on our left. It seems improperly charac-
terised by Milton, ' the smooth Severn stream '
('Comus,' v. 825). He has given it a fitter epithet
in his invocation of rivers ('Miscellanies,' p. 307, ed.
Warton), where he calls it 'Severn swift.' Spenser
calls it 'the stately Severn,' and couples it with the
' storming Humber,' and says that both of them
' honoured ' the Thames as their ' principal.'

> And let their swelling waters low before him fall
>   *Fairy Queen*, Book IV Canto 11, Stanza 30.

Its stream seems everywhere more rapid, eddying,
and turbid than the Thames, though perhaps the
description given of it by the old monkish historian
William of Malmesbury may be rather overdone. He
says : ' There is in it a daiely rage and fury of the
waters, which I know not whether I may call a gulfe
or whirlpoole of waves, and the same raising up the
sands from the bottom, winding and driving the same
upon heapes, cometh with a forcible violence,' &c.
(Camden's ' Britannia,' Gloucestershire).

.   .   .   .   .   .

Tuesday, July 18.—Left Llangollen after breakfast. It is but thirteen miles from Ruthin; but
here, again, *hoc iter ignavus,* &c., I knew I should
have many hills to encounter, and particularly one
of a mile and a half long, and very steep, a little
way from Llangollen. I had never ascended such
a hill as this; and I could not have achieved it
if I had not had light web traces with me, to
fasten on the other horse occasionally. These were
of the greatest use during my journey. Where the
country was hilly, and sometimes in heavy roads, my
servant rode with them fastened about his horse; so
that it took but a minute or two to put them to the
chaise shafts and take them off again. This hill is
called *Bwlch Rhiw Velen* · very high steep hill over
you, on the left, and on the right a deep valley. But
the road itself is wide and good : it winds round the
side of the mountain. Stopped at a little pot-
house—called, in Welsh, *Tafern Dwrch* ; Anglice,
'The Turf Tavern'; sign, The Cross Foxes—by
way of dining. The fare was such as might be
expected. There was nothing to be had but some
last slices off a bone of mutton, which Jonas was
obliged to assist in cooking; bad bread, bad cheese
—nothing tolerable but the ale. But I was amused
by conversing with the fat old Welsh landlady in
the kitchen, and with observing something of Welsh
cottage manners. She spoke English very well,
though in the Welsh accent and tone; and told

me a long story about Castle Dinas Bran, and the
bloody battle of two giant brothers and the moving
intercession of their mother Corwena (whence the
name of Corwen, near Llangollen) to reconcile them,
—all which she related with the appearance of full
belief. She said she had a book about it, and apologised for not doing the story justice, adding, that
' it was very fine in the Welsh.'

From Tafern Dwrch I proceeded to Llanvorog, my
journey's end, where I arrived a little after 5 o'clock.
This village is a continuation of Ruthin, separated
from it only by a handsome stone bridge over the
Clwyd (pronounced Cluid).

The country from Tafern Dwrch till you come
to the Vale of Clwyd is wild and dreary. The first
view of that rich vale was a cordial to the eye. Yet
it was not exactly what I expected. I had formed
an idea of a narrower, closer, more Matlock-like
valley; and in general such little vales please me best,
as being more uncommon, more romantic, more like
a picture, and more soothing to the mind (at least to
mine) by the idea of deep repose and retirement from
the world. The Vale of Clwyd is wide, open, cheerful, &c. I don't know that a better idea of it can be
conveyed than by the description of Camden, as it
appears in the old simple English of his translator
Philemon Holland. ' We are now come into the very
heart of the shire (Denbighshire) where Nature, having
removed the hilles out of the way on both sides, to

show what she could doe in a rough country, hath
sp ed beneath them a most beautifull pleasant vale,
reaching 17 miles in length from north to south, and 5
miles or thereabout in bredth, which lieth open onely
towards the sea and the cleering north wind ; otherwise environed it is on every side with high hilles, and
those from the east side as it were embattled For
such is the wonderfull workmanship of Nature, that
the tops of these mountaines resemble, in fashion, the
battlements of walles.   This vale, for wholesomenesse,
fruitfulnesse, and pleasantnesse, excelleth.   The vale
itselfe, with his greene meddowes, yellow corne-fieldes,
villages, and faire houses standing thicke, and many
beautifull churches, giveth wonderfull great contentment to such as behold it from above.   The river
Clwyd, encreased with beckes and brookes resorting
unto it from hilles on each side, doth, from the very
spring head, part it in twaine, running through the
midst of it '

The Clwyd at this time was, like most of the
rivers I saw in N. Wales, only a little stream scarcely
hiding the stony channel it dimpled over.

As shallow streams run dimpling all the way —*Pope.*

A few stepping-stones would have been bridge
enough for it in the state I saw it in during my stay
at Llanvorog ; but in the winter and after great rains
it is a different thing.   The town of Ruthin (which is
pronounced Rîthin) has nothing remarkable about it
but the beauty of its situation and the ruins of the

old Castle. It stands upon a pretty steep hill, down which you go to the bridge, and to Llanvorog. In thir, and in all the principal towns in N. Wales, one is shoved back half a century by the appearance of the buildings (in general), and particularly of the shops, which look mean and shabby. The imitative spirit of improvement has not yet got so far; yet it has only to travel from Shrewsbury, about 40 miles. At the top of the town there are cheerful and comfortable-looking houses, and a handsome church, with a very fine green-and-gold iron gate into the churchyard, that was not well in tune with things about it. The situation of the Castle, the walks about it, and the venerable and picturesque appearance of its ruined gateways, arches, walls, towers, &c., well mixed up with old trees and bushes, and tumbled about upon broken ground, with a fine view of some part of the town under it, the gardens, the bridge, and the village of Llanvorog—all this pleased me much, and I often enjoyed this scene in my walks. So little, however, is left of the Castle, and the ruins that remain are so near the ground, that it is not seen in a distant view of the town, or very little of it.

These mountains, with a long chain of others to the right of them, form the east wall, as one may call it, of the Vale of Clwyd; though, indeed, its direction is not exactly N. and S., but rather a little north-west from Ruthin, and the chain of mountains forms a curved line. Ruthin is about half a mile from Mrs.

Hughes's house, and these mountains—the tops of
them—must be, I think, two or three miles from Ruthin, yet the summits are seen in Mrs. Hughes's garden,
over her house. They appear much nearer than they
are. Their height, their fine, waving, irregular outline, their breaks and openings, the perpetual variety
of their appearance with respect to light and shadow,
not only from the different positions of the sun, but
from the passing clouds, the shadows of which were
continually sweeping over them—all this, which was
in a great measure new to me, afforded me amusement every time I went out of the house But what
was most curious, and, as far as I recollect, quite new
to me, was the effect produced by clouds hanging on
their tops and rolling down their sides. At first the
effect to me was that of a great smoke occasioned by
burning something on their tops Sometimes the
clouds hung below the summit, and the outline of the
summit itself was distinct. A circumstance rather
pleasing to one's imagination is that all these hills are
personified, as it were, by distinct names. One is
'Voel Vama,' *i e.* the mother mountain (Voel is
mountain ; Vama, mother—sometimes Mama, for
the initial letters of words in the Welsh language
are varied, according to the termination of the preceding word, but by what rule Mr. Hughes could not
tell me) ; another ' Mole (or Moel) Arthur,' on the
top of which there are some traces remaining of an
entrenchment, said to have been made by the renowned

Prince Arthur. (The meaning of the word Mole or Moel I forget)

Wednesday, July 19.—(The day after my arrival at Llanvorog) Went to dine with Mrs Humphreys at Upper Eyarth, a very fine elevated situation on the side of one of the mountains, about two or three miles from Ruthin Fine view of the vale, and an excellent specimen of Welsh hospitality, and plenty and un-ceremonious welcome.

Thursday, July 20.—Mr. Hughes took me in his whisky up a long and steep hill, which is the road to Chester Near the top we had a noble view of the whole Vale of Clwyd, Denbigh, St Asaph, and the sea beyond it, closing the north end of the vale. We saw also a very high mountain at a great distance, which Mr Hughes took for Snowdon, but I think there was some doubt about it afterwards. This was, indeed, a capital prospect of the wide, staring kind. After this ride we went to dine with Mrs Wynne, at Lower Eyarth, very near to Mrs. Humphreys, of Upper Eyarth, but situated lower down on the hill, and, to me, far pleasanter, and with much more snug beauty about it. It is sheltered by fine woods upon broken ground, diversified by rich shade and romantic rocks intermixed, overhanging a deep and narrow little rocky valley, with a small but bustling stream, and mill, &c. We saw more of this spot (called, I think, the Eyarth Rock) afterwards. Mrs. Wynne is a lady of good fortune, an heiress, and very hospitable.

I never heard anything more extraordinary than the melodies of her speech. They are compounded of the peculiar tones of the Welsh language, aided by some personal tones of her own. The beginnings of her sentences sometimes were so loud and shrill and sudden as to make one almost start. I can't say of her, as Ovid says of Io, when she was turned into a heifer,—

Pertimuitque sonos, propriâque exterrita voce est.

Friday, July 21.—A charming ride on horseback with Mr. and Mrs. Hughes to Pontychel Bridge— a delicious little, romantic, hermit-like valley, under the rich long woods of Lord Bagot. We rode down hills that were very like old broken stone staircases.

Saturday, July 22.— Drank tea with a Mrs. Jones at Ruthin. I was much amused with the extreme Welshness of the good lady. Walked after tea to see the ruins of the Castle, and the Bowling Green, beautifully situated on part of the ground where the Castle stood.

Sunday, July 23.—Went with Mr. Hughes to Llanvorog church. Service and a sermon in Welsh by a Mr. Williams, usher of the Grammar School at Ruthin, who, as my Mr. Hughes told me, reads extremely well. My curiosity was much gratified by hearing the sound of the venerable old language well pronounced. It was not at all harsh or uncouth to my ear. The guttural sounds were soft, *dérobés*, and inoffensive. I never saw a more attentive and decent

congregation   One thing caught my ear in the service ·
I found that *and* was *ag*—the Latin *ac*, with the
c turned into *g*   I could not help thinking of Sir
Hugh Evans, in the 'Merry Wives of Windsor,' and
his *hig, hag, hog,* &c. (Act. IV., scene 1)

Tuesday, July 25 —In the morning walked with
Mrs. Hughes and two Miss Newcomes (Elizabeth and
Maria, daughters of the Rev Mr Newcome, of Gresford, near Wrexham, formerly of Queen's Coll Cam)
and Daniel, to the Rev Mr. Roberts's, at Llanryth
(pronounced Llanreēthe), a sweet retired spot, just the
thing I like.[1]   A comfortable and convenient house ,
a garden very well laid out in the modern taste, well
planted, well varied, with a clear stream running close
to it; a handsome stone bridge of a single arch, which
has a very good effect in the scenery about it ; rising
hills, woods, meadows, and the great mountainous
screen closing the view.

Mr. Roberts was of St. John's College, Cambridge,
in my time, and well acquainted with my friend,
Archdeacon Leigh, who, with his wife and daughters, had visited him at Llanryth not long ago.   I
rather wondered that I did not recollect something
of him.

Thursday, July 27 —I can't omit a charming
evening walk with Mr. and Mrs. Hughes, the Miss
Newcomes and Daniel in some woods called *Coed Mar-*

---

[1] Il y a des lieux que l'on admire, il y en a d'autres qui touchent,
et où l'on aimeroit à vivre.—*La Bruyère.*

chan. 'Coed' is Welsh for wood ; 'Marchan' is the
name either of the high hill on which the woods hang,
or of a farmhouse situated on its side, I forget which.
A wild, solitary, shady, up-and down walk, views
glimmering through the trees, and a rustic bath in
the rock, closely screened by trees—a most tempting
bathing-place for hot weather.

Friday, July 28.—Went to Denbigh with Mr
Hughes, Mrs Watts, Maria Newcome, and Daniel—a
very pleasant ride.   Passed through Denbigh to see a
famous place of the Rev. Dr. Middleton at Gwayny-
nog.   The situation is fine, but the place had been
neglected and looked uncomfortable.   The walks
were not in good order, &c.   One part of our walk
about the park was delightful, rising and falling and
winding through rich hanging woods and by a little
murmuring stream, forming here and there little
cascades, which are heard where they are not seen.
Dr. Johnson made some stay at this place when he
visited North Wales with the Thrales in 1774, and
we saw an urn erected to his memory in a part of this
walk close to the little stream, which we were told
was his favourite spot.   There was an English com-
plimentary inscription on the urn, but it was something common, and I forget it, as I do also the name
of the possessor of this place at the time when Johnson visited it,[1] for it had but lately become the property of Dr. Middleton.   Workmen were busy about

---

[1] I believe it was Jol n Middleton, Esq.

the house, which is not large nor grand, but something
better—snug, habitable, comfortable—such as one
may wish to live in without being romantic.   But the
pleasantest part of this morning's expedition was our
walk back to Denbigh   In one part of the park we
were considerably nearer to Denbigh than the house
is, where we had left our vehicles.   Therefore we sent
them on and walked.   Nothing could answer better.
The Castle lay in our way.   Denbigh Castle was the
finest ruin of the kind that I had then ever seen.   Its
bold situation, perched upon a high rocky hill, has a
striking effect at a distance.   We passed close to its
old walls and towers, one of which I think hangs nearly
as much out of the upright as the Falling Tower at
Bridgenorth.   A fine rich gateway remains, with a
figure in a niche over it, whether of Henry Lacy, Earl
of Lincoln, who built it, or of Edward I., from whom
the earl held the town by grant, I know not.   (I hope
no antiquary will read this journal.)[1]   From the rock
on which the Castle stands we had a fine, extensive
view of that end of the Vale of Clwyd, and a sort of
bird's-eye prospect of the town of Denbigh under us.
The other end of the vale, however, is, I think, more
rich and beautiful than this end of it, and I believe it
is generally reckoned so.   This end seems more open
and extended ; the other has more of the closer
beauties which painters like.   It divides itself more

---

[1] I find it is the figure of Edward I., but I scorn to erase my ignorance or forgetfulness.

into choice little landscapes Among other distant
objects which we examined with our glasses from the
Castle hill was a fine house built (or building) by Mrs.
Piozzi, who, in my opinion, has not shown a good
taste in changing the Welsh name of the place to a
fine Italian name—*Brin bella*.[1]

We had not time to see much of the town of
Denbigh. The entrance from Ruthin is up a steep
street that put me somewhat in mind of East Hill
in Colchester, but· the ascent is steeper, straiter, and
much longer. There are some good houses on it.
We dined at the Bull Inn, and returned to Llanvorog
by tea-time.

Saturday, July 29.—Walked to Mrs. Wynne's at
Lower Eyarth, and after a little rest and refreshment
(for it was a hot day) we rambled about the Eyarth
Rock, viewed all the romantic scenery of the woody
walk, and descended, not without some difficulty, into
the little dale I mentioned (p. 202), which, indeed, is
only like a great fissure in the rock. At the bottom
runs a little stream in a rocky channel, which, in one
place, loses itself underground for a little while, the
rock forming a sort of low arch over it. In most of
these Welsh rivulets there is but little water (except
after rain), but the little there is tries to make all the
fuss and bustle it can. Where it can hardly be seen,
it contrives to make itself heard in that continual
watery rustle which forms an accompaniment so

---

[1] *Brin* is an eminence.

suited to such sequestered and poetical scenery. In
order to do this it seldom spreads itself equably over
the whole channel, narrow as that is. It chooses a
still narrower channel on one side (leaving the other
part almost dry), where the rocky bottom will afford
it more irritation by obstacles, and give it an opportunity of endeavouring to make itself of some consequence by struggling, cascading, foaming, &c Daniel
scrambled down into the bed of this little river, hunted
it into its subterranean passage, and, by the help of
the dry part of the channel, made his way through it
and emerged on the other side. We had lost sight of
him for some time ; we called, but he did not answer;
we were growing a little anxious about him when,
turning round, we saw him, to our great surprise,
sitting quietly perched upon the high ridge of craggy
rock above us that shuts in the little valley. This
was, altogether, one of those pleasant and uncommon
scenes that are not soon forgotten · Daniel invisible
at the bottom of the river ; we bawling to him to take
care of himself ; Mr Hughes amusing himself with
rolling great pieces of stone down the steep, rocky
bank, to hear the echoing splash of them in the water ;
some of the ladies holding the flaps of his coat, that
he might not fling himself down the precipice with the
effort of throwing ; some resting upon rocky seats at
different heights ; some climbing, scrambling, slipping,
&c. ; and all of us at last got safely to Daniel, seated
coolly upon his ridge. It was the middle of a warm

day, and we had a long walk still to take. The ladies were indefatigable, and scorned to get into Mr. Hughes's whisky, which came to meet us. I was glad to make use of it, for the walk to Eyarth, and the ramble in the woods and dale after it, had tired me pretty well.

So much for our charming little excursions in the neighbourhood of Llanvorog during my residence of twelve days there. We should have set out a week sooner upon our tour in Carnarvonshire, &c., but that we waited in hopes of my brother joining us at Mrs. Hughes's and setting off with us. This, however, he was not able to do ; and on Monday, July 31, we set out with good hopes of seeing him at Llanrwst, where we were to sleep the first night.

Monday, July 31.—Set off, about 10 o'clock, for our Welsh tour: Mrs. Hughes and I in my chaise ; Mrs. Watts and Mr. Hughes in his whisky ; Daniel T. on horseback. Our road was through Clokanak and Llanfihangel, to Kerrig-y-Druidion (pronounced Kerigidridion)—Anglice, Stones of the Druids. A monument of that kind remains on some of the hills near the place. We dined at a miserable ale-house in this village, 12 miles from Llanvorog. Nothing can be more dreary and comfortless than this place, and, indeed, the whole ride to it—bleak, barren hills, and execrable road. My wheels did not fit the ruts, which, in some places, were deep. I gave up my coachmanship to Daniel, and mounted my horse.

Somewhere on the left, about Llanfihangel, I think, I observed a little, deep, woody dell, that looked the more tempting for being surrounded with nothing but bareness and dreariness. The smoking roofs of cottages appeared here and there among the trees. I longed to dive from the bleak hills we were upon, into this soft, tufty hole. After our dinner, which consisted of eggs and bacon for the rest of the party, and toasted cheese for me, we pursued our way to Llanrwst, through the villages of Kerniogge and Capel Voelas. We were now in the great Irish road, which is excellent   The entrance into the vale of Llanrwst, or, rather, into the road by the edge of it, was grand and striking, far beyond anything of the kind that I had ever seen. I lamented, however, that the evening was too far advanced for us to see distinctly ; though, perhaps, that very indistinctness might contribute to the effect. What the eye loses, the imagination gains. Obscurity is grand. If you could see what you see, you would, perhaps, see less. The next day we saw the vale distinctly. It had more of beauty, less of sublimity, than in our dusky entrance. It had more resemblance to Matlock than to anything I had seen before, but upon a far greater scale, and with the addition of the great mountains that bound the view, rising above each other, and some of the highest confounding their outline with the clouds. The bottom of the vale, which we looked down into from our road, in a kind of bird's-eye view,

is a wide, rich-looking level ; all the contrast of
which garden-like appearance with the rude, romantic,
tossed-about scenery around it, has, to me, a pleasing
effect. The beautiful light bridge, with the river and
background of woody mountains, are fine features in
the picture. We put up at the Eagle. This stage
(from Kerrig-y-Druidion) is 14 miles.

Tuesday, August 1.—Rain, but it cleared up. My
brother R and his son John arrived to breakfast.
‘ O qui complexus,’ &c. Set out, after breakfast, with
a guide to see some waterfalls. We passed over the
famous bridge (supposed to have been built by Inigo
Jones), turned to the left, under the beautiful hanging
woods of Gwydyr Park to Pont-y-Pair, a narrow,
picturesque, stone bridge, with a fine rush of water,
foaming over great stones, through the arches. (I
have a notion that this bridge is also called Bettws
Bridge). This was one of those things that I had
never seen before but upon canvas Yet it was
nothing to the next fall we came to, called, I believe
(for none but Welshmen can be sure of Welsh names),
Rhaidr-y-Wennol.[1] We went a mile or two to the
right after passing Pont-y-Pair ; dismounted, and
walked down to a meadow, where our guides helped
us to scramble down to a great rock in the river,
where we sate, close to this tremendous fall of water,
the foam of it spitting in our faces, and the noise
seeming to grow louder and louder, and the water

[1] *Rhaidr*, I think, means fall or cascade. *Wennol* is a swallow.

more and more angry, every moment we stayed. There is something very fine in the sensation of being perfectly safe, while death is staring you in the face within an inch of your nose. 'It is sweet,' says Lucretius, 'to sit and see others in danger, while you are safe.'[1] But it is sweeter to see danger that nobody is in, so near as to give you the feel of being in it yourself, while this imaginary and voluntary terror is immediately turned into pleasure by the consciousness of perfect safety. Even a Twining may face danger in this manner. In our way to this water-fall by the river side, on the left, we passed a very beautiful cascade, that came glittering down from the very top of a high, soft, woody hill, in little streams and bursts, here and there. We returned to Pont-y-Pair, and went on in the road that turns to the left of it (after passing it from Llanrwst), to see two other falls. One was at Pont Arleder (a bridge over the river Leder, I believe); not quite so fine as that of Pont-y-Pair, but through larger masses of rock. Hence, by a road almost impassable for a carriage, to another famous fall called Pandy-Pen-Machno. This rather disappointed me; I thought it inferior, by many degrees, to the Rhaidr-y-Wennol, which should have been seen last. But, really, I was so extremely fatigued before I got to it, that I had neither eyes left to see, nor judgment to compare. Yet we were told that this fall was generally preferred to the

---

[1] 'Suave mari magno,' &c. lib. ii. init.

other, because (as the guide told me) that river (the
Machno, I think) never wants water ; but the river of
the Rhaidr-y-Wennol does, except after rain ; and
at this time there had been much rain. Another
reason of preference may be, that this fall divides
itself into different falls, separated by rocky projec-
tions, which the painters may regard as more picturesque, and fitter for their purpose. The other fall
(Rhaidr-y-Wennol) is all one mass of white foam ;
the height not great ; but, if I recollect rightly, there
was one sheet of foam over another. It is a fall, I
think, of the whole stream ; but the fall is broken,
though without any visible separation by rocks either
laterally or perpendicularly. This excursion should
be made on horseback. The road is not fit for a
carriage in the *détours* you must necessarily make
out of the high road to get at these falls. Our morning's ride was not less, I believe, than 15 or 16
miles ; we were out six hours. I was excessively
fatigued. We should have been contented to have
returned home directly from Rhaidr-y-Wennol ; or,
if we had determined to see all that could be seen, we
should have kept the best for the last. Nothing will
bear an anti-climax less than seeing things. But
nothing is so common as to spoil pleasure by intemperance. I experienced upon this tour, that one may
be sick with seeing as well as with eating. Yet the
intemperance of the traveller is the most natural and
pardonable of all sorts of gluttony. We see what we

never saw before, what we probably may never see again, what is highly worth seeing, and what we have but a very limited time to see. It is 'now or never;' and so we cram sight upon sight, for the sake of seeing everything, till we really find considerable comfort in sitting down and seeing nothing. I once said that I would write a book with this quaint title: 'The Christian Epicure; or, the Luxury of Temperance.' How tired one may be (at least, I often have been) even with things excellent in their kinds, and things of which one is fondest! All entertainments— plays, concerts, operas, oratorios—are too long for me. Music has been, and is, one of the greatest charms of my life, and nothing has fatigued me oftener. But, in travelling, as I said before, one has not time to be temperate. This I take to be the great defect of these tours, or seeing-schemes in general. To have seen comfortably, sufficiently, and quietly all that we saw in this tour through Carnarvonshire and Merionethshire, would have required three weeks or a month at least. We allowed ourselves but eleven days. The exquisite beauties of this charming vale, and the variety of uncommon, and what one may call poetical, scenery, which we passed through in our morning's ride, I shall never forget; but I should deserve to forget it if I attempted to describe it. On the whole, it stands foremost in my memory as the most capital thing we saw in the whole excursion. But, though it must strike every spectator in some

degree, it can be thoroughly relished only by those
who have learned to see things with a painter's eye ;
what Ælian calls τεχνικὰ ὄμματα— technical eyes, or
such as an artist has. We say, ' Such a one has a
good ear, a bad ear, no ear.' Why should the expression be confined to the sense of hearing ? Why
not say, also, ' He has no eye,' &c. The meaning
would be the same as in the other application of the
phrase, in which it is not meant that a person is deaf,
but that he hears without pleasure ; hears the sound,
but does not hear the beauty of the sound ; or, at
least, hears it very weakly in comparison with others.
Many people, in the same manner, ' have eyes and
see not.' How many men who see a beautiful view
just as their horse sees it ! It is painted upon the
retina of both. Hutcheson would have said that they
have the external sense without the internal. Ælian[1]
tells a story of Nicomachios the painter. He was
viewing—fixed in admiration—the famous Helen of
Zeuxis. A man who had no eye for such things
asked him what it was that he so wondered at. ' You
would not ask that,' replied the painter, ' if you had my
eyes.'[2] I like a verse in the book of Proverbs : ' The
hearing ear, and the seeing eye, the Lord hath made
even both of them.' But I would not answer for it
that Solomon meant all I understand by it. I should
not leave Llanrwst without noticing the beautiful

[1] *Inquiry concerning Beauty*, &c., sect. i., art. 10, p. 8.
[2] *Var. Hist.* lib. 14, cap. 47.

situation of the churchyard, close to the bank of the Conway, broad and clear, the bridge, the bold, woody projection of the Gwydyr rock on the opposite side, mountains beyond, &c. We slept here two nights, and on

Wednesday, August 2, after breakfast, we proceeded to Conway, where we dined (Bull Inn). A charming ride of twelve miles by the side of the Conway ; the road excellent. At Pont Dôlgarreg, a little bridge about four miles from Llanrwst, over a rivulet that runs across the high road into the Conway, we were unexpectedly delighted with a cascade, the most beautiful of the beautiful kind that I had seen. The stream was not large, but fell from a great height. At the top was one smooth, clear, shining, transparent sheet of water, that appeared to have no motion, in the midst of little foaming bursts. There were four or five of these down the side of the mountain, and a good bustle of water at the bridge. Cottages perched up and down, at different heights, improved the scenery. I enjoyed this the more, as I had heard nothing of it, and saw it at my ease, from a good turnpike road, without going an inch out of my way.

As you approach Conway, the river widens into an estuary ; the prospect, too, widens, and changes from the narrower scenery of the vale to a grand, varied, and interesting view of the castle, with its round towers and long lines of ragged battlements sloping to the river ; the town, the sea, the Isle of Anglesea,

and the bold promontory called the Great Orme's
Head, mixed up with some softer features of rich
hanging woods, &c. The effect of the castle and old
fortifications is striking at a distance But the best
view of all this is from a garden, or cultivated ground,
belonging to Mrs. Holland, in which we walked before
dinner. The town is well paved, and has a clean and
cheerful appearance. We looked at a curious old
house just by our inn, which, we were told, belonged
to the Wynne family : a Greek motto over the door :—

’Ανέχου καὶ ἀπέχου (sustine et abstine)

A very good moral lesson, to be sure ; but it was ill-
timed, for we were all very impatient for dinner, and
not at all disposed to practise abstinence Here we
heard the only good harper that I met with in North
Wales. At Llanrwst we were pestered with modern
tunes, ill played, upon a noisy harsh instrument. The
bard at Conway was an old blind man, John Smith.
His harp was full-toned and mellow, and he played,
con amore and expressively, the old national tunes.
We admitted him into the room after dinner. The
modest old man, when we commended his playing,
shook his head, ‘No, no, I cannot please myself.’
He had taken lessons formerly of Parry, of whom
he spoke with enthusiasm. It is very odd, but
it is true, that his playing affected me, even to
tears. It would not at all have had this effect
upon me in England. Local associations did the

business. A Welsh bard, playing in Wales, at
Conway, historical and poetical recollections, the
melancholy simplicity of the tunes themselves, their
antiquity, the Welsh soul which the old blind man
seemed to put into them—all these circumstances,
and perhaps others, caught hold of my fancy, and,
as they say, set me off. All the other harping I
heard in North Wales was bad, fit only to interrupt
conversation, and spoil one's dinner. We walked
about the ruined apartments of the castle, which are
worth examining. After dinner we went on to
Bangor (fifteen miles), where we slept (Eagle). The
passage over the side of Penmaenmawr is the great
feature of this ride. A steep precipice on your right,
from which you look, almost perpendicularly, about
100 yards down to the sea ; a vast height of mountain, rising almost perpendicularly over your head, on
the left—this mountain side covered with very large
loose blocks of stone, which threaten to fall down
with every blast of wind, and which, if they did fall,
as you are passing, must, in all probability, crush you
to atoms. These circumstances are the ingredients
which, all together, compose that mixed and awful
sort of pleasure which this famous pass gives the
traveller. What must this passage have been before
the turnpike road and the strong parapet wall on the
right existed ! Even now there is some danger, from
the loose crags of rock, when the wind is stirring.
Every now and then a mass of stone comes thunder-

ing down, bounds across the turnpike road, knocks down the wall, and rolls down with a tremendous dash into the sea beneath. We saw several places in the wall that had been newly repaired after accidents of this kind. I should suppose that no one would venture to travel that way in a high wind. We stopped to drink tea at a very comfortable, neat house at Aber, a little village about six miles from Bangor. Here we were told of a waterfall two miles off, but it was too late to walk to it. I was glad we did not attempt it, as we saw it in great perfection the next morning.

.   .   .   .   .   .

When we arrived at Bethgelert, we found that the Dean of Christ Church had for some time taken up his quarters at the small and only auberge of this little retired village, and occupied the whole house. Fortunately he was gone out, and we had the use of his room, but the only dinner we could get was eggs and bacon, potatoes, and toasted cheese. They who grumble at such a dinner as that are not fit to travel. A tour to Salt Hill [1] or Hampton Court would suit them better. Before dinner we walked about three quarters of a mile up a little, close, and sequestered valley by the side of a river rushing over large stones and fragments of rock ; and forming, a little

[1] Salt Hill (a little over three miles from Windsor) will be remembered by many as the hamlet to which the Eton boys formerly went in the 'montem' procession—'ad montem.' The mount, however, is but a small one; the procession was abolished in 1847.

way higher up, a pretty and gentle cascade of the whole stream, which steps down, as it were, from the smoothest and most glassy quietness, into the rocky and obstructed channel a little way beneath it. Near this cascade is a picturesque little wooden bridge, which we past, into verdant meadows, where haymakers were at work. This little valley differs from that at Aber in having more of the beautiful mixed with solitary grandeur. It seemed to have more of Arcadia and pastoral life about it. There was, of course, more of contrast, for the mountains, which screened it closely on each side, were very high and steep, and with a bare, black, and rugged surface. We were the more pleased with this vale from having never heard it mentioned. Your true tourist seldom sees anything but what has been seen by every tourist before him. These routine-seers follow one another like a flock of sheep :

> E ciò che fa la prima, e l' altre fanno,
> Addossandosi a lei s' ella s' arresta,
> Semplici e quete, e lo imperché non sanno.
>
> DANTE, *Purg.*

They generally travel with a catalogue in their pockets of things to be seen, with which they have been favoured from the journal of some fashionable tourist ; and whatever Sir Tasteless Seeall has recommended as worth seeing must be so—whether a beautiful valley or a copper mine, a waterfall or a stocking-machine, the top of a mountain or the bottom

of a coal-pit, it is all one. I remember very well
that the late Bishop of Lincoln, Thurlow, came many
years ago, and long before he had any thoughts of
episcopacy, to pass a day at Twickenham. We
walked about, and I was the cicerone ; and while we
were seeing Pope's house and gardens, and many
other places and views well worth seeing, he expressed great satisfaction at having that day seen a
thing he had often heard of, but never seen before—
the Red Lion at Brentford. With respect, however,
to us Welsh tourists, it must be owned that if we
have taste, we have not time to go out of our way
for the chance of unseen beauties. But I have no
doubt that if any man of real taste for the beauties
of nature could stay a month at Llanrwst or Tan-y-
Bwlch, he would find out many delightful nooks,
many little romantic vales, and, where the ground is
so perpetually varying, many happy and picturesque
combinations of mountain, valley, wood, and water,
equal, if not superior, to those which are commonly
known and admired.

.   .   .   .   .   .

Thursday, August 10.—After breakfast we set out
for Llanvorog, where we arrived by dinner-time,
heartily tired, and jolted almost to dislocation, by ten
miles of very rough and narrow road, with stony ruts
too narrow for my wheels. Luckily, we broke neither
our necks nor our carriages. I never felt a finer
arrival in my life ! a more complete enjoyment of

the luxury of being quiet : of sitting still and letting pleasure come to one, instead of having to run after it—of having no horses to order, nowhere to go, nothing to see but what might be seen by only opening one's eyes. Some philosophers make the happiness of Heaven to consist in ' sitting still and wanting nothing.'[1] It is a happiness not exactly calculated for man ; but there are times when we do get a little taste of it, and in this world there is very little danger of our getting too much of it. Motion, say these philosophers, implies imperfection. I am much more sure that there is a great deal of imperfection in motion—the motion of travelling, at least ; and this very imperfection, and the fatigue arising from it, were the sole causes of our enjoying so much the opposite and more divine pleasure of sitting still ; for in a day or two I found myself as human and imperfect, and as ready to encounter the inconveniences of travelling for the sake of its pleasures, as I ever was.

Monday, August 14.—We all dined with the Rev Mr. Roberts at Llanryth. A very pleasant visit. If I were a poet and had a mind to personify ' retired Leisure,' I would not make him

—— in *trim* gardens take his pleasure

(which always offends me in Milton's description). I would put him in Mr. Roberts's garden at Llanryth ;

[1] See Harris, *Philosophical Arrangements,* p 448, &c , and Hermis, 359, Note E.

with his companions 'calm Peace and Quiet,' but not 'spare Fast, that oft with gods doth diet,' but never, I believe, with Mr. Roberts of Llanryth—at least he was not there to-day, for we had an excellent dinner.

Tuesday, August 15.—After dinner I took my leave of Llanvorog, and set out for Wrexham, on my way home. I never left any place with stronger wishes that I might one day see it again, and see it as I left it. In this mixed world the recollection of three weeks passed in a way perfectly to one's satisfaction, and without any want, any defect, any drawback of circumstances unpleasant to one's tastes and fancies, is a valuable thing. But what was happiness to me (and, I believe, to all the party at Llanvorog) would, I know, be miserable *ennui* to many people. I am so constructed that I really do not think I could be equally happy in any place more exposed to good company—to the artificial manners, the *gêne*, the etiquette, the buckram ostentation, rivalry, insipidity, and vanity of polished and moneyed life. It was a great comfort to me that I did not meet with a single fine lady or fine gentleman all the time I was in Wales, except, indeed, one gentleman who affected to be fine, and was the only disagreeable person I saw. Mr. and Mrs. Hughes accompanied me as far as Wrexham, in their way to Mr. Newcome's at Gresford, where I, also, had been very kindly invited to pass a few days. But I had been absent so long that

I was seized with such a pining after home as the Swiss soldiers are said to be subject to in foreign service when they hear the *Ranz des Vaches*—the old simple tune, which they had been used to hear and play upon their bagpipes when boys, keeping their cattle in the mountains of their native country.

. . . .

August 18.—Proceeded from Rugeley to Lich-field, about seven miles from Rugeley and nine from Wolseley. I put up at the ' Talbot,' which had been recommended to me, but it was not the right sort of house ; there is great want of room in it, and I was obliged to dine in my bed-chamber, and there was a difficulty made about my having any bed in the house the next night. The accommodations, however, were very well, and the people very civil. But it is rather a market-day house, for farmers, riders, &c. I believe I should have gone to the ' George' or the ' Swan.' My intention was to sleep here only one night, and proceed on my journey the next morning. But finding, upon inquiry, that my old friend Egerton Leigh, Archdeacon of Salop, and one of the Residentiaries of the Cathedral, was now here, I determined to prolong my stay. The pleasure of seeing an old and intimate friend, whom I had not seen for near forty years, and whom I never expected to see again, was not a thing to be given up for anything less than necessity.

As soon as I had dined, I called at his house in

the Close. He was at home. I refused to send in my
name, but desired to speak to him. He came to me
into the passage, peering and scowling at me, with
his hand over his eyes, as much as to say, What
can the fellow want ? I made him a sneaking
bow. 'Sir, I hope no offence, sir. Knowing the
benevolence of your character, and your generous
disposition, I take the liberty to wait upon you. I
am a clergyman, sir, and in distress, as you may see,
sir, by my coat.' 'Oh, sir, indeed I can't. I have
many such applications as this ; but I know nothing
of you, and I never attend—I make it a rule——'
'Sir, excuse me ; but knowing your character for
learning, and particularly, sir, your skill in the Greek
language——' ('O, sir, that is all—I know nothing
of the matter.')—'I thought I might take the liberty to
solicit your encouragement for a little [pulling papers
out of my pocket]—a little treatise I have written upon
the Greek language, sir ; the title of it, sir, is Τί ἐστί
σοι τ' οὔνομα.' [This, I took it for granted, would
open his eyes, as it alluded to a circumstance which I
thought he could not have forgotten. Being once at
a play with him, in a crowded pit, a woman, who
thought herself incommoded by him, was angry.
Leigh, with that sort of humorous folly that was
peculiar to him, turned to her, with his grave, im-
movable face, and asked her Τί ἐστί σοι τ' οὔνομα ?
('What's your name ?'), which made her still more
angry. I had no doubt, therefore, that the recollec-

tion of this, and the improbability of such a title for
a book, would discover me immediately. But it did
not ; he answered]—' No, sir, indeed I can't say anything to it—you must excuse me.' ' Sir, I am very
sorry. I thought that, as I once had the pleasure of
knowing you——' ' Knowing me, sir ? Indeed I don't
know ——.' I then smiled, said nothing, but held out
my hand to him. He would not, take it but shrunk
back, and declared he had not the least knowledge
of me. Then, at last, I was obliged to discover myself. ' What !' quoth I, ' don't you know TWINING ?'

I shall never forget his change of countenance. I
could compare it to nothing but the effect of the sun
breaking out suddenly from a dark cloud. What
followed is easily conceived. I had a hearty welcome,
and a hearty laugh. Nothing could answer better
than my trick. It was a fine dramatic ἀναγνώρισις, or
discovery ; and there was also a sort of περιπέτεια, or
revolution with it ; a sudden change of fortune in me,
from a beggar to a friend. He introduced me to his
youngest daughter, Theodosia. Mrs. Leigh and his
eldest daughter were from home. I drank tea and
spent the evening with them. His daughter played
a lesson or two upon her piano, and after supper we
sung a few glees, and talked of old times, and Cambridge days, with a great deal of that peculiar sort
of enjoyment which such unexpected meetings of old
friends, after a long absence, commonly afford, and
for which, I think, we have no name in our language ;

but the French express it happily by *épanchement—
épanchement de cœur*, what Pope calls, poetically
enough, ' the flow of soul.'

I looked, of course, at the house in which Johnson
was born—a house with pillars at the corner of the
Market-place, now, I think, a grocer's shop. I also
visited the famous large old willow-tree, which Johnson, they say, used to kiss when he came to Lich-
field. It stands in a pleasant pathway across the
meadow, from the Close to the other end of the town.
The weather was rainy while I was here, which interrupted me in my prowlings about the place. Lich-
field will not bear any comparison with Worcester,
except for its Cathedral and the Close, which is open,
handsome, and pleasant. I don't know a more for-
lorn-looking place than the Close at Worcester, and
the Cathedral is a poor thing in its way

The monuments erected to Dr. Johnson and
Garrick, in the Cathedral, disappointed me The
inscription upon Garrick's commemorates ' his dramatic powers '—a striking impropriety in such a
place. Nobody has more respect and admiration
than I have for such dramatic powers as Garrick's ;
but to talk of them in a place dedicated to the
Supreme Being ; to connect them in this manner
with the ideas of death and another world—surely
this is improper and indecorous, if anything is so.
When a man's virtues and good qualities are enu-
merated upon his monument, it must always be

understood as saying, 'As he was a good man, we hope he has gone to heaven.' But the idea of a man's being the more likely to go to heaven for his dramatic powers is perfectly absurd.[1]

PROJECTED VISITS.—TYRWHITT'S 'CHAUCER.'

To his Brother.

Colchester, November 22, 1798.

No really ; my thoughts about my next summer's travelling were only general foreseeings. I have no fixed scheme. I have now and then felt a wish to go to Plymouth (Gandy) and Boconnoc (E. Forster) and Mr. Welch's ; these would make one tour, and be all novelty to me—a great matter—besides seeing old friends worth seeing. Indeed, at my time of life, seeing friends, of the most intimate and valuable kind, grows to be a more important and precious gratification than seeing places. When one can consolidate the two pleasures, it is well. The most intimate and the most—what shall I call it ?—the most congenial, the most coincident friend I have, except yourself,

---

[1] This passage will doubtless remind the reader of some remarks in a very similar spirit made by Charles Lamb in his Essay 'On the Tragedies of Shakespeare.' He says : 'Taking a turn the other day in the Abbey, I was struck with the affected attitude of a figure which . . . proved to be a whole length of the celebrated Mr. Garrick. Though I would not go so far, with some good Catholics abroad, as to shut players altogether out of consecrated ground, yet I own I was not a little scandalised at the introduction of theatrical airs and gestures into a place set apart to remind us of the saddest realities.'

certainly is J. Hey. We are both far down the hill, and both, I believe, greedy to get as much of each other while we are capable of enjoying each other and our common tastes and amusements as we can. Passenham attracts me in every possible way. I therefore set my visits there high in the scale of itinerary foreseeings ; and cheek by jowl stands Isleworth. So that if the Doctor should propose my visiting him next summer, I should be very well disposed to give up more distant ramblings for the sake of enjoying his company and yours (with your &c.) in two quiet abidings at Passenham and Isleworth. But alas ! when do you abide quietly at Isleworth ? You can't think how pleased I was with that part of your letter that tells me how you have of late enjoyed yourself there. Go on ! you ought to enjoy yourself, and unless you do, others cannot enjoy you.

Mr. Tyrwhitt's edition of Chaucer's ' Canterbury Tales' is a book that I delight in ; his accuracy is so satisfying, and the tales themselves so amusing, so manner painting, &c. I wonder why I have never read them through !—I suppose the trouble of Glossary-hunting stopped me. But I have read many parts with great pleasure. His ' Poore Persone of a Toun ' is an exquisite thing.

SOME BROTHERLY COUNSEL.

To his Brother.

Colchester, Dec. 10, 1798

Dear Brother,—Thanks for your sociable and close-written letter. This day, if I mistake not, your *otium cum dignitate* is at an end for the present. But mind, you are to return to it as soon as you can. What you say about your *future*[1] *abidings* at Isleworth, and the use you mean to make of your good, and able, and willing substitutes, *Lieu-tenants*, &c. likes me well. I never knew you talk so well upon that subject before. But keep to it. Let us have no backslidings. You never 'looked back' when once you had put your hand *to* the plough , don't look back when you have taken your hand *off* Yes, yes, you did express yourself 'modestly enough' I know nobody more unlikely to do otherwise Don't you know that I have often *loved* you for being too modest ? (I meant to have sent this letter to-night, but I have not time to finish It must go to-morrow So good-night)

Tuesday, Dec. 11.—You talk very fairly about your 'supposed love of a bustle,' and I am quite ready to allow that it would not be fair to bring the necessary 'bustle' in which 'necessary business' has

---

[1] The relief which my Grandfather *did* obtain from his sons in the Strand was in no slight degree counterbalanced by his election as an East India Director.—R T. 1881

engaged you as a proof that you love a bustle, as matter of *choice* and inclination. But I did not suppose Hughes to mean that, nor did I take his expression in the rigour of the *letter*, but a man who like H. (and me) loves *still life* (perhaps *too* well), calls everything that is not that a bustle, &c. Suppose he had said (I believe it was all he meant) 'he certainly loves *active life*, I as certainly retired and quiet life.' (Or if you think *loves* too strong, put *prefers.*) I think also, that in saying this, he had in his mind not your own necessary bustles of business, but the bustles of other businesses in which you have often engaged with so much ardour, and certainly, as I am sure we *both* of us think, with so much credit to yourself. Do I blame you for it? Not I, indeed ; far from it. Often have I heard you something *like* blamed for these voluntary labours added to those of your business ; I always dissented And as to your earnestness in whatever active part you *do* take, you are over candid indeed, when you seem willing to allow it to be called a *fault.* I heartily wish, 'every part of your constitution' were as good as that. . . . Keep your heart where it is and what it is. And whenever it pushes you into a crowd, don't be ashamed of it, but go on, and look back with a smile of pity upon us idle fellows gaping and stretching on our beds of roses. I am not able to throw any light upon your dark line of reading. I have gone but a little way in that line. I never read Warton. I think it would be too much for me. I have always thought that his criticism has too much Antiquarianism in it. I know of no book to recommend. You have got beyond me in these matters. I have found Cotgrave's Fr. and Eng. Dictionary a useful book, in the old line. I have lately met with an odd vol. of a book that seems useful and well done. It is ' Histoire de la Littérature d'Italie' (a subject very interesting to *me*) 'tirée de l'Italien de M. Tiraboschi, et abrégée par Antoine Landi,' &c. Berne, 1784. 3 volumes 8vo. When you go near Elmsley's I wish you would ask whether it is a book of good character and whether they have it. The original Italian book I see is in Payne's *last* catalogue, 9 v. qu. £4 14 6. I would rather have the French abridgment, besides its being (I suppose) cheaper. This moment comes to me your letter by I. M. O ho ! what ! is my sister on *my* side about Wales ? Then will I be more saucy and more positive than I have been. Go to with your doubts and your wisdom. I will write again very soon. Though you have not time to *write* letters now, you *have* to *read* them.

FRIENDLY BANTER —CHAUCER IN BLACK LETTER.

To his Brother.

Colchester, April 10, 1799.

I am very glad my correspondent is come to life again. Silent (except a little note or two) for a whole month! A French lady said of a very ugly man, ' Ce monsieur-là abuse trop du privilège qu'ont les hommes d'être laids.' I could almost apply it to you and the privileges of business. I should not, however, have let you alone so long if the daily expectation I was in of hearing from you had not made the probability of my letters jostling yours upon the road every day increase. It was very near being the case now. I seem to have a great many things to say. Let me begin to say them. I cannot conceive you to lose your relish for reading by business ; I should think it more likely to increase it, though what Lord Bacon calls the 'viscosity' of ' human nature' may, just at first, make a man's legs stick a little if he tries to skip too nimbly out of the one into the other. What seems most natural of all, to a man with my notions, tastes, and habits, is, that the indulgence of a relish for reading and study should spoil the relish for business. But this is no more than if I should say, surely a man who likes a nectarine can never endure an olive ; when I myself detest an olive, and therefore am no judge in the case.

Your black-lettered Chaucer!—why do you read him in the black letter? What a painstaking, thorough-paced, thorough-stitched man you are when you set about anything! I never read a black-lettered book in my life. And then, you have read all Juvenal and all Quintilian! I am quite an idle fellow, a *fainéant* compared to you! If a literary life had

been your lot, you would have done great things.
If you take this for Mrs. Slipslop's figure of *ironing*,
you are much mistaken   I never was more in earnest.
I just now recollected that I was possessed of one
black-letter book.   Shall I send it you ?   It is ' The
Secretes of the Reverende Mayster Alcais of Pie-
mount ; ' and upon opening it the first receipt I saw
(for it is a book of receipts and nostrums) was ' to
make one have a good stomache that hath a naughtie
one,' which I take to be your case.

A VISIT TO CAMBRIDGE—FEARS OF A FRENCH INVASION.

To Dr. Hey.

Colchester, October 31, 1803.

And you are so lively and *éveillé* at ten o'clock
at night that you can sit down to write a letter !   If
I were to attempt such a thing I should be fast asleep
before I got to the third line.   My utmost exertion
after supper is playing upon my piano ; but I soon
play myself to sleep, and sometimes find myself playing on, mechanically, my own fancies, when I am
everything but fast asleep, and fancy is quite out of
the question.   I do believe that the soul is all over
the body, and some of it in one's finger's ends.   But
let me come to answering and biography.   And as I
am very far, just now, from being in my usual state
of still life, biography shall come first.   My going to

reside at Cambridge a month or six weeks of this winter, will be quite an epoch in my life ; and I don't see why my flight from Colchester may not make as good an era or Hegira to date from as the flight of Mahomet from Mecca. After some deliberation with myself and with my brother R. it is settled that on Monday next, November 7, which is my Notley tithe day, instead of returning hither the next day as usual, I shall take myself and my money on from Braintree to Cambridge. My brother R. came to Cambridge on Wednesday last, to make a little stay with Daniel on his way to St. Faith's, for which place he sets out on Thursday next. They have taken for me a convenient and comfortable lodging, consisting of a sitting-room and closet-bedroom opening into it ; and, which I like, up-stairs. My landlady (I know not at present her name) is the cook of Peter House ; lives in Trumpington Street, opposite to the ' Cap ' that was. I am to pay 12*s.* a-week, she finding me linen, &c., and as for eating, with a College cook I can be at no loss. I meant to have boarded where I should lodge ; but my brother could make nothing of that plan that would do. College rooms, even if I could have got them, would not have suited my tenderness and habits of domestic comfort and attendance. I suppose you will not ask me why I leave Colchester. I leave it because I am afraid to stay in it. Many have left, more are preparing to leave it, though I myself think there is very little danger, yet I should be very uneasy to stay here and run the risk And if I stay till the moment of alarm upon the coast, I may not be able to get away at all unless I walk away with a knapsack on my back. Now, though I do not go to Cambridge for pleasure, yet I think it will be a pleasure and an amusement to me to pass a little time in the bosom of my old nursing mother, rubbing up old and pleasant recollections, &c I shall feel safe; I shall feel academic; have access to libraries, and hear a little music. Now, my dear Doctor, what a clever thing it would be if, instead of taking J. M.[1] to Oxford, you were to change your plan and bring her to Cambridge! You would not visit Crotch indeed, but Professor for Professor you could visit Hayne; and, *quod rerum omnium primum est* (to me), I should be of the party.

There are two delightful little *Cavatine*, a hot summer one, and a cold winter one. The last J. M. would sing charmingly. With the accompaniment well played, the effect, I believe, would be delightful. If Crotch goes no further than disapproving some whimsical imitations, I can agree with him. There are some capital fugues (not servilely Handelian) which, I should think, must please him. Sorry Hayne is retrograde Poor H. Wightwick! It was not her, I think, that I accompanied at R. H.'s If

---

[1] 'J M.'—Jane Missenden, afterwards Mrs. Carnaby, wife of Dr Carnaby, a professor of music She was in her best days a most exquisite singer of Handel's music.'—R.T. 1881.

the French should come to Cambridge, who knows but I might run away so in *Piel*[1] as not to stop and look back till I reached your door at Passenham, breathless, and with my hair standing on end. Your Marquis of Buckingham says, I am told, that Cambridge is not safe ; because, if the French should land upon the Norfolk coast, it would be on their road to London (a man is just come to put up a telegraph upon my steeple). I should relish your Boccacio party (so the name is written in my edition of the ' Decamerone,' Venezia, 1590). That good fool, Francesco Berni, in a very ludicrous character and account of himself which he has introduced in the middle of his burlesque poem (' Orlando Innamorato di Boiardo rifatto'), goes farther than you propose ; he will hear no news at all.

LIFE AT CAMBRIDGE.

To Dr. Hey

King's College, Cambridge, November 2, 1803

DEAR HEY,—*Corpo di Bacco!* King's College ! Keep your precious eyeballs in their sockets. I lodge[2] at Mrs. King's, that's all. She is Anne King ; and upon all her plates A. King She is cook of Peter House ; but that, I believe, I told you. I did not tell

---

[1] ' Piel,' a Hebrew conjugation implying earnestness, exertion, &c

[2] He spent the winter at Cambridge owing to the apprehension so much felt at Colchester of a French invasion.—R T , 1881.

you, I think, that her daughter is a very pretty, pleasing girl. Nothing can be more comfortable and convenient than these lodgings a pretty, neatly-furnished sitting-room, up one pair of stairs; a small dormitory, but with a window to shave at, bureau, drawers, pegs, &c., and a glass. A neat tent bed, like my bed at Passenham, shelves, &c.; a door near my fireside, and at the other end, where the bed is, a sliding panel in the wainscot, to lay the bed-room, if I please, into the sitting-room, which I do please, every night, both for air and for warmth , and, indeed, for room, the wainscot being too near the bed to leave any convenient *ruelle* to get into bed from. My dinners come from the College kitchen. I have what I like, and live very comfortably. Plenty of good Cottenham, and the very best beer that I ever drank in my life. The house is next to St Botolph's church, on the Pembroke side. Daniel and I are, of course, good neighbours, and in the evenings (when not engaged) we read together. Our present book is ' Cic. de Oratore,' and we are now in the jokes. I have great pleasure in reading with Daniel; his judgment is so unshackled, and so fairly his own, and his relish for humour so good. I had a very good journey hither, in postchaises; Frank with me, by leave of his colonel I sent him back by coach (there is now a Cambridge and Colchester coach three times a-week) on Thursday the 10th. Though I could have done without him, he was of great use, in looking after my luggage upon the road, and in settling me here, constructing my bed, and making the people acquainted with my ways and likings.

The foregoing letter is the last of the series which has been selected from an extensive Correspondence for the present publication. The interchange of letters, however, was continued for some months later, even to within a few days of Thomas Twining's death ; but the later ones from him, though showing unfailing powers of mind and tranquillity of spirit, tell but too distinctly the tale of increasing infirmities, fore-shadowing the end, which was so near at hand. On August 6, 1804, he died in peace.

MISCELLANIES.

The Boat.[1]

(An imitation of the ' Dedicatio Phaseli ' of Catullus.)

Nunc recondità
Senet quiete !

The boat which here you see, my friends,[2]
Sharp as a needle at both ends,
A bean-shell[3] for my wife and me,
Deep loaded when it carries three ;
A mongrel thing—pray take a view—
Between a boat and a canoe :
This *boat* (for we will not defame,
Nor quarrel for an empty name)
Protests and vows, and, if you'll have it,[4]
Is ready to make *affidavit*,
That she's the fleetest little thing
That ever flew on wooden wing[5]
On Father Thames[6] she calls to say

---

[1] The Parsonage at Fordham had a moat or piece of water of sufficient capacity for a small boat which was built for him at Twickenham, and became a source of much amusement.

[2] ' Phaselus ille quem videtis, hospites.'

[3] *A bean-shell.*] The vessel called *Phaselus* is supposed to have got its name from its resemblance to a species of pulse called *Phaseolus*, which is the term applied by botanists to the *kidney*-bean　See Millar

[4] ' Ait fuisse navium celerrimus '

[5] ' Remigio alarum,' Virg. passim　If wings may be called oars, oars may be called wings. Sails are compared to wings—' velorum alas,' Virg. Oars have more similitude to wings, by their *position* and their *action*

[6] *On Father Thames &c.*] ' Et hoc negat minacis Adriatici,' &c.

If any bark e'er cut its way[1]
So swiftly through his liquid glass,
But she, with ease, would quickly pass,
And, whether urged by oar or wind,[2]
Would scuddle by, and leave behind.
This Father Thames will say , and she
Full many a day has joy'd to see
How oft the god would rise and stare,
Shake from his eyes his weedy hair,
To her in pleased attention turn,
Leaning his elbow on his urn,
And smile, and look so grimly merry,
To see his fav'rite little wherry,
And mark how deftly over all
Her floating sisters great and small,
With all their oars, and all their sail,
The plaything boat would still prevail ;
While watermen the dashing oar[3]
Have oft suspended as they swore,
And surly bargemen, forced to toil
In stream becalm'd, and smooth as oil,
Have spit their quids with many a ' Blast 'em,'
And ' d—d the bean-shell,' as she past 'em.

---

[1] ' Neque ullius natantis impetum trabis
Nequisse præterire,' &c.
[2]   . . . 'sive palmulis
Opus foret volare, sive linteo.'
[3] Collins's ode on the death of Thomson ·
' And oft suspend the dashing oar
To bid his gentle spirit rest.'

R

All this the god will vouch for true,[1]
This all his creeks and islands knew :[2]
Each little ait, if you will ask it,
That ever gave the world a basket ;
His verdant banks on either side,
The villas trim that grace his tide ;
Proud *Richmond*,[3] that with tow'ring brow
Lifts from the mirror clear below
Its woody side (where, haply, she,[4]
Though now a boat, was once a tree) ;
Beneath, green meadows, and at top,
Benches that often rest a fop ;
Tall staring houses in stiff rows,
With trees before as stiff as those ;
Poetic *Twit'nam*, and its grot,
Where Pope caught cold when he was hot—
A thing (for let it have its due)
Exceeding pleasant to look through ;
But Fate, alas ! too near had placed
The Dæmon dire of *Anti-taste*[5]—
Green *Teddington's* serene retreat,

[1] ' Tibi hæc fuisse et esse cognitissima
       Ait phaselus.'
[2] ' *Insulasve* Cycladas.'
[3] ' Rhodumve nobilem,' &c., &c.
[4] ' Ubi iste, post phaselus, antea fuit
       Comata sylva.

[5] The poet *Thomson* used to call the old Lord Radnor ' the
Dæmon of *Anti-taste*.' Mr. Pope's grotto, about which such a fuss was
made by himself and his friends—and still more, a temple of shells
that stood near it—were childish things that would have been more
properly placed in his neighbour s garden.

For philosophic studies meet,
Where the good Pastor, *Stephen Hales*,[1]
Weigh'd moisture in a pair of scales,[2]
To ling'ring death put mares and dogs,
And stripp'd the skin from living frogs
(Nature he loved, her works intent
To *search*, and, sometimes, to torment ') ;
Long, rattling *Brentford*, old and new,
And shady *Ham*, and courtly *Kew*—
All these, her boatship says, declare
Her tale is true, her claims are fair.
Nor this, she says, her *only* praise ;
She vows too that in all her days,
Howe'er the changeful wind might blow,[3]

[1] Rector of Teddington.

[2] See his *Vegetable Statics.* Dr. H. was an ingenious man, and made some useful experiments ; but those here alluded to are such as can be justified by scarce anything short of necessity, or, at least, a strong probability of their leading to discoveries highly importing the good of mankind. Curiosity, or the vague expectation of discovering something or other, is not a sufficient excuse for putting any living creature to a painful death ; but it is generally the real motive, though men are glad to conceal from themselves their cruelty by giving it a better name, and talking about the good of mankind   See Vol II of the *Vegetable Statics*, where several mares, not fewer than twenty dogs, and several other animals, were put to death in the most painful and lingering way ; and he was particularly interested in flaying the skin off the bellies of live frogs, to see the motion of their blood and muscles. (Page 59.) And see the dedication to Vol. I., where he speaks of it as one great use of studying the works of Nature, that they ' convince us of the benevolence and goodness of their Author.' One would not expect such an observation to be followed by such experiments

[3]   . . . ' læva sive dextera
        Vocaret aura,' &c.

R 2

However rough the stream might flow,
She never made one Fribble flinch,
One tim'rous lady scream or pinch ;
One oath her master never swore,[1]
One moment wish'd himself ashore
' But, ah !' she cries, 'how changed the scene !'[2]
Troy *was*—and I, alas ! *have been*[3]
Nor swifter ev'n myself can glide,
With ev'ry aid of wind and tide,
Than happy days and youthful prime
Fly down the rapid stream of time.
I, who was born on *Thames's* shore,
In Thames's stream first dipp'd my oar,[4]
Each feat forgot of youthful praise,
Doom'd, the remainder of my days,
Instead of *Thames's* ample flood,
To paddle in a pond of mud ![5]
Fair Twit'nam, gay-frequented scene
Where ev'ry evening deck the green
Bag-wigs, and swords, and negligees,
Midst herds of cows and clumps of trees
(Such things as make Dame Nature stare
And wonder what could bring 'em there)

[1]   . . . 'tot per impotentia freta
Herum tulisse. . . .
Neque ulla vota litoralibus Deis
Sibi esse facta.'
[2] 'Sed hæc *prius* fuêre,' &c.
[3] 'Troja fuit,' Virgil.
[4] 'Tuo imbuisse palmulas in æquore.'
[5]   . . . 'hunc ad usque *lim, idum lacum* '

Exchanged for Fordham's rustic nook,
The lonely walk, the silent book,
The quiet lane, so grassy green,
Where waddling geese alone are seen,
Save now and then a clown you spy
With vacant whistle lounging by :
Rare as th' eccentric comet's blaze,
The prodigy of passing chaise.—
The antique Pars'nage, undermined
By rats, and shaking to the wind ;
Ducks, chickens, goslings, pigs, and cows,
The Parson, and the Parson's spouse ! '[1]

[1] 'Gemelle Castor, et gemelle Castoris '
(*i.e* Castor, and Castor's brother).

A CORRESPONDENCE BETWEEN MR. TWINING AND
PROFESSOR HEYNE.

To Professor Ch. G. Heyne.

Cum ex fratre meo, vir præstantissime, intelli-
gerem se Aristotelis περὶ ποιητικῆς versionem meam
cum dissertationum ac notarum qualiumcumque
apparatu ad te, primo quoque tempore, jam a prelo,
quod aiunt, madentem, mittere constituisse, oravi
statim eum, et, quod semper fuit in omnia mea vota
propenso vereque fraterno animo facile impe-
travi, ut ne me occasionem hanc ultro oblatam
arripere vetaret, vel levi adeo hoc munusculo haud
levem illum testandi, quo te suspicio, honorem et ob-
servantiam. De specie, ratione ac consilio satis in
præfatione dictum, de incommodis et molestiis quibus
in eo perficiendo premebar, parum, pro eo quod res
erat ; sed profecto ejusmodi querelis in publicum
quodammodo παρατραγωδῶν prodere non sustinui. In
secessu ruris degenti, nulla mihi bibliothecas vel
publicas, vel privatas quidem paulo lautius in-
structas adeundi facultas : tantum abfuit ut de
codicum manuscriptorum ope vel somnio quidquam
cogitarem. Intra arctos bibliothecula meæ parietes
omnis mihi necessario res erat gerenda. Ad hoc
adversa valetudine sæpe interruptum opus : sæpe
fastidio quodam ac languore animi depositum seu

verius abjectum ; vixque tandem jam fracto, et quasi
refrigerato impetu, iterum in manus sumptum. Vides,
vir humanissime, quam sedulo id agam ut mihi quasi
viam muniam ad indulgentiam tuam facilius conse-
quendam, siqua præsertim in iis quæ ad textum, quem
vocant, ac linguæ Græcæ rationes, spectant, offenderis,
quæ ἀκρίβεια tuæ minus satisfecerint. Hoc enim te
persuasum velim, neminem esse cujus judicio plus
quam tuo tribuam, aut cui magis quæ scripsi probare
exoptem. Hoc unum te, tot tamque gravibus officiis
et studiis occupatum ac districtum rogare ausim,
siquid forte tibi annotationes meas cursim evolventi
gravius a me delictum in oculos incurrerit, ut de eo
me benigne monere ne graveris.

Perjucundum est quod accepimus, te de nova
Homeri editione adornanda cogitare. Hanc vero occasionem nactus, mihi temperare nequeo, quin de
uno versiculo emendando quid mihi dudum in
mentem venerit tecum communicem. Semel vero me
(quo facilius veniam dabis) in Homero legendo pru-
ritus emendandi solicitavit.

Στεῦτο δὲ διψάων, πιέειν δ᾽ οὐκ εἶχεν ἐλέσθαι.—Od. λ. 583.

Sic legitur hic versus iis saltem quæ mihi ad
manum sunt editionibus. Sed στεῦτο, στεῦται, de cujus
verbi notione ac vi satis ex ejus usu constare videtur,
quidquid tandem de etymologia sit statuendum, semper, quantum equidem scio, apud Homerum cum

verbo infinito construitur, non, ut hic, cum participio solo : e g.

Στεῦται γάρ τι ἔπος ἐρέειν.—Il. γ. 83.
Στεῦται γαρ νηῶν ἀποκόψειν ἄκρα κόρυμβα.—Il. ι 241.
Στεῦτο γὰρ ῾Ηφαίστοιο πάρ' οἰσέμεν ἔντεα καλά —Il σ. 191.
Στεῦτο δ' ὅγ' ἀμφοτέρων ἀποκοψέμεν οὔατα χαλκῷ —Il. φ 455.

Et aliis in locis. At vix dubitem το πιέειν a loco suo prava interpunctione divulsum, et legendum esse :

Στεῦτο δὲ διψάων πιέειν. Οὐδ' εἶχεν ἑλέσθαι.

Quam conjecturam meam tuo judicio libenter per-mitto. Est autem quod nobis gratulemur omnes quotquot sumus emendatores, nos haud Zeleuco legumlatori ὑπευθύνους esse ut hariolationes nostras non nisi *collo* in *laqueum inserto* præferre liceat. Sed nolo te diutius hac mea ἀδολεσχίᾳ demorari. Vale, vir doctissime atque optime, neque in eorum habere numero me dedigneris, qui summam erga te obser-vantiam et voluntatem non modo cognitam sed pro-batam etiam—siqua fieri possit, ac res ita tulerit—spectatamque esse cupiant. Datum Colcestriæ d. 26 Feb., 1789.

To Dr. John Hey (with a copy of the above).

P.S.—I did not think to have endorsed my Latin, but I must. We have had a young violinist here, one Galott, who wants employment somewhere. He thought of Colchester. I told him that would never do.

He wished to make a concert, I believe to discharge his wine bill, poor fellow. He says he was nine years in Italy and educated in the Conservatorio at Naples. He left Italy ten years ago. He seems, by questions I asked him, to speak truth ; but why he is so embarrassed I know not. He has a great deal of neat execution, farther I cannot say. He now tells me he means to go to Cambridge and wishes me to recommend him. I promised to mention him to you, and ventured to tell him he might call on you.

———

TRANSLATION OF THE REV. THOMAS TWINING'S LETTER TO PROFESSOR HEYNE AT GOTTINGEN.

Rev. T. Twining to Prof. C. G. Heyne.

Most Excellent Sir,—Having been informed by my brother of his intention to send you, as soon as published, a copy of my Translation of Aristotle on the art of Poetry, with my Dissertations and Notes, such as they are, I immediately requested his permission (which, with his usual kindness he readily granted), to avail myself of so favourable and tempting an opportunity of testifying my high regard for you by begging your acceptance of this trifling gift.

The nature and plan of the work I have stated sufficiently in the Preface ; the difficulties with which I had to struggle were in reality much greater than

I have stated ; but I could not bring myself with a sort of tragical gravity to lay a formal detail of them before the public. Living, as I do, in a very retired situation, I could consult no public library, nor even any private one that was tolerably well stored ; much less could I so much as dream of profiting by the aid of manuscripts. All my resources were necessarily confined within the contracted limits of my own library. In addition, my task was often interrupted by ill health ; was often laid, or, I should rather say, thrown aside in disgust or depression of spirits, and resumed only with impaired energy and abated warmth. Observe, my good sir, how industriously I wish to secure the way to your indulgence when you meet with anything, especially relative to the Text and the Greek language, to which your accurate judgment cannot assent. Of this I would have you thoroughly assured, that there is no one to whose judgment I attach greater weight, or whose approbation I more earnestly desire. The only favour I venture to beg of you, engaged as you are in a variety of important duties and pursuits—is, that should your eye in a hasty perusal, detect any great errors in my remarks, you will condescend to point them out to me

We have heard with the greatest delight of your intention to publish a new edition of Homer. Nor can I refrain on this occasion from communicating to you the correction of a single verse which long since occurred to me. That I may the more easily obtain your indulgence, I assure you it is the only instance of my being seduced, whilst reading Homer, by the love of emendation.

This conjecture I gladly consign to your judgment. We emendators have—everyone of us—great reason to congratulate ourselves on being no longer amenable to that law of Zeleucus—that no one should offer any conjecture without a halter about his neck.

But I will no longer detain you thus idly. Farewell, most learned and excellent sir, and disdain not to reckon me in the number of those who not only wish their esteem to be known to you, but upon every occasion to give every possible proof of its sincerity.— *Colchester,* 26 Feb., 1789.

Professor Heyne's Reply.

Beâsti me munere, vir doctissime, quo vix memini aut vidi aliud jucundius magisque gratum a longo inde tempore mihi obtigisse. Soleo enim libello Aristotelis tribuere tantum, ut, lectione præstantiorum omnis ætatis scriptorum subactum ingenium *sensu* quidem omnis præstantiæ et pulchritudinis facile perfundi, requiri tamen præterea putem judicium subtile in caussis, cur quid placeat vel displiceat reddendis, in constituendis boni pulchrique generibus, gradu, discrimine: ad judicium autem hoc seu parandum seu

acuendum nihil salubrius, nihil potentius, esse libelli
Aristotelei lectione et interpretatione diligentiore :
quem etiam aliquoties lectione publica enarravi adeo-
que ipso usu cognovi, vel ipsa interpretatione animum
ad subtilitatem fingi, siquidem philosophi sententias
sententiarumque nexum velis assequi satis : cum propter argumenti naturam tum propter philosophi acumen,
imprimisque per orationem concisam et salebrosam :
quæ ad sensum meum omnia a te, vir præstantissime,
præclare adumbrata video[1] Quum enim ipse difficul-
tates multas magnasque in hoc libro enarrando, plus
quam alius quis senserim, non miraberis si me adspectu
tui libri ingenti voluptate percussum dixero Inspexi
et percurri illum, et, animadversa incredibili segete
bonarum rerum, reservavi eum primo recensui litte-
rario, quo popularibus meis notitiam præclari hujus
libri in Recensibus Gottingensibus litterariis proponam :
tum vero novis lectionibus super ipso libro Aristoteleo
futura hieme habendis.   Continget itaque forsan aliquando ut liceat tecum agere pluribus de uno alterove
capite.   Valde delectavit me opera a te posita in
notione *imitationis* accurate constituenda. Turbavit
illa vox non minus populares meos : verum nos adscis-
cimus aliam vocem eamque minus in fallaciam et
fraudem inducentem, *Darstellung*,[2] ut Poesis sit ars,

---

[1] Meaning, I suppose, in pp. 6, 7 of my preface.

[2] *Dar* is German for *there* and *stellen* (infinit.) is *to place, put, settle* : so *Darstellung* is exhibiting, &c.; and poetry in the German language is not an *imitative*, but a *there-putting* art This comes to the Greek ἐνάργεια.

quæ sensibus res subjiciat, representet, exhibeat oratione ad consilium illud, seu ad finem accommo-datissima, seu ea oratione qua sensus potentissime moveri possunt.

Nos Germani philosophiæ in Academiis doceri solitæ partem constituimus $\alpha i \sigma \theta \eta \tau \iota \kappa \dot{\eta} \nu$ qua sensus boni, pulchri et venusti a caussis suis repetitur, ejusque seu monendi seu regendi, h.e. dijudicandi ratio tra-ditur. Comparatio, quam instituere licet eorum, quæ a Britannis, Gallis, et Italis, super hisce rebus disputan-tur, cum iis, quæ a popularibus meis in multis libris enucleata sunt, delectationis et utilitatis habet pluri-mum : etsi enim multa incommoda habet hæc littera-rum nostrarum ratio in Germania, ut exterorum sermonem nemo paullo politior ignorare possit, com-pensatur tamen hæc molestia utilitatibus haud medio-cribus.

Utinam otii satis atque annorum tantum, contingat ut in Homero perficere liceat quod in Virgilio saltem sequutus sum. Enimvero in vita versor negotiosa et curarum varietate districta inque eo ætatis gradu constitutus sum, ut mihi potius de conveniendo mox in inferis Homero quam de eo recensendo cogitandum esse videatur. Interea progrediar quousque progredi licuerit. Fata viam invenient.

Emendatio tua, Od. λ. 583, est et elegantissima et judicio meo verissima · equidem et ante videbam esse subintelligendum $\sigma \tau \epsilon \hat{v} \tau o$ (sc $\pi \iota \epsilon \epsilon \iota \nu \ \delta \iota \psi \acute{a} \omega \nu$) Nec vero incideram in emendationem tam paratam et facilem

cujus laus tibi debetur · quemadmodum hæc insigni
tuæ humanitatis existimatio et predicatio, cum me
hominem tibi nomine duntaxat notum et a fratre poli-
tissimo viro commendatum, et munere tam præclaro et
litteris humanissime et elegantissime scriptis ornaveris.
Quoties in libro hoc evolvendo versabor, memoria tui
recurret jucundissima, daboque operam ut siquid sit
quod ex nostris terris gratum tibi et jucundum esse
possit ad te perferendum curem. Vale, vir humanissime, et quod semel judicium de me suscepisti tuere.
Scr. Gottingæ d. xx. April. 1789.

Constitueram litterulas simul ad fratrem tuum
amantissimum dare Nunc intelligo tuis verbis hoc
idem me consequi posse, si exoravero te ut meo nomine ei salutem reddas gratumque animi sensum
declares pro beneficio hoc, quo mei notitiam tibi injecit.
Aliam salutem ejus conjugi lectissime impertias rogo
nomine uxoris meæ.

Redditæ sunt litteræ tuæ 26 Febr. scriptæ xii. April.

TRANSLATION OF PROFESSOR HEYNE'S LETTER TO THE
REV. THOMAS TWINING.

Ch. G. Heyne to the learned Thomas Twining, greeting.

I know not, most learned Sir, that I ever received
a more agreeable and acceptable present than that
with which you have favoured me. So high is the
opinion I entertain of this work of Aristotle that I

think it requisite, in order to understand it, that the reader should previously have acquired a ready perception of whatever is excellent and beautiful by studying the best writers of every age ; that he should besides be able to assign with precision the causes why we are affected with pleasure, or the contrary ; to determine the different kinds of excellence and beauty, their gradations and distinctions ; that nothing tends so powerfully to produce or improve this faculty as the diligent study and explanation of this very work of Aristotle, which, having sometimes made the subject of a public lecture, I know, from my own experience, that whoever with a view to explain endeavours to understand the thoughts of the philosopher, and to trace their connection, invigorates the power of his own mind ; and this not only from the nature of the subject and the depth of the philosopher, but particularly from the conciseness and abruptness of his style , all which qualifications you clearly possess in a most eminent degree.

And since no one could be more sensible than myself of the great difficulty attending a translation of this book, you will not be surprised if I assure you that the sight of yours afforded me the highest gratification.

No sooner had I received it than I gave it a hasty perusal, and having perceived so choice and abundant a harvest, reserved the further notice of it for the next number of the ' Gottingen Literary Review,' in

which, as well as in the course of lectures which I
shall deliver in the ensuing term upon that very work
of Aristotle, I shall recommend your admirable book
to the attention of my countrymen.   It may happen,
therefore, that I shall, at some future opportunity,
discuss some passages with you at large.

I was particularly pleased with the pains you have
taken to fix the proper sense of *imitation*, a word that
had not less confused my countrymen than yours,
though we had used a word less calculated to puzzle
and mislead—viz., *Darstellung*.

If I live and have leisure, I hope to achieve the
same for Homer which I have done for Virgil.   But
I lead a busy life, distracted by a multitude of cares,
and am of an age, too, that seems to admonish me
rather to think of meeting Homer in the other world
than of being his editor.   Meanwhile, I shall proceed
as I can—'Fata viam invenient.'

Your emendation of Homer is most elegant and
most just.   I was myself aware that the word στεῦτο
(sc. πιέειν διψάων) was to be understood, but had not
hit upon that clear and safe emendation, the credit of
which is entirely yours.

I am most sensible of your polite attention in
doing me the additional honour of accompanying so
noble a present with a letter written with so much
taste and elegance to one known to you only by
name, and through the kind recommendation of your
accomplished brother.

As often as I am occupied in the perusal of your book, I shall think of you with the greatest satisfaction, and make a point of sending you any publication in this country which I think may prove worthy of your acceptance. Farewell, most worthy sir, and continue to preserve the good opinion you entertain of me

Written at Gottingen, April 20, 1789.

LONDON : PRINTED BY
SPOTTISWOODE AND CO , NEW-STREET SQUARE
AND PARLIAMENT STREET

S

Printed in Great Britain
by Amazon.co.uk, Ltd.,
Marston Gate.